Coping with

THE DEATH OF A BROTHER OR SISTER

Ruth Ann Ruiz

The Rosen Publishing Group, Inc.
New York

Published in 2001 by The Rosen Publishing Group, Inc.
29 East 21st Street, New York, NY 10010

First Edition

Cover photo © Ira Fox

Library of Congress Cataloging-in-Publication Data

Ruiz, Ruth Ann.
Coping with the death of a brother or sister / by Ruth Ann Ruiz.—
1st ed.
p. cm. — (Coping)
Includes bibliographical references and index.
ISBN 0-8239-2851-9
1. Grief in adolescence—Juvenile literature. 2. Bereavement in adolescence—Juvenile literature. 3. Loss (Psychology) in adolescence—Juvenile literature. 4. Brothers and sisters—Death—Psychological aspects. 5. Teenagers and death—Juvenile literature. [1. Death. 2. Grief. 3. Brothers and sisters—Death.] I. Title. II. Series.
BF724.3.G73 R85   2001
155.9'37—dc21
                                                                00-011751

Manufactured in the United States of America

About the Author

Ruth Ann Ruiz is currently an educational consultant and writer in Tucson, Arizona. She completed both a bachelor's and master's degree at the University of Arizona. She also founded La Escuela Educational Services, which now provides assistance to small charter schools as well as students who are in need of intervention teaching strategies. *Coping with the Death of a Brother or Sister* is her first book.

Acknowledgments

There were so many people who gave me their support as I worked on this book. I wish to thank each of them for encouraging me to pursue my dream. A special thanks goes to the staff of Children to Children, who provided direction for me as I began my research.

Thank you, Kristy, for checking out material from the university library. Thank you, Yvette, for returning my late books to the college library. Thank you, Kerry, for watching your brother.

Thank you, Joey, for making me laugh and allowing me to write. Thank you, Eva Landry and Adrienne Segal—without you, I would still be dreaming.

Contents

Introduction

You don't choose them; they are given to you. You may not have asked for them, but they are yours. You were put together in the same family because your parents selected each other as mates. You choose your friends, but you don't have the chance to approve or disapprove of your siblings. You are given your brothers and sisters.

You may act out many different roles with your siblings. At times, you are in competition. You also work together as partners. From a very early age you share your space and your belongings. And you share love and hate.

The death of a sibling is the end of a special relationship. With the death you will experience a great deal of pain. At times you may have many regrets. You may also wonder, "Why me?"

Together, siblings share a set of memories—both happy and sad—that are not shared with parents or friends. These memories are different. They are very special.

You shared a secret language with your sibling. It was unique, and your parents did not share it. There were looks across the dinner table, like the one that said "Dad is annoyed . . . " or "Let's get out of here fast!" There were the hand signals that told you when your sister needed you to rescue her from a boring telephone call. Or the times when your brother sat with you while you were feeling sick. Now your brother or sister has died. And when you look across the room, you see emptiness. Your secret language has been silenced.

You shared your bedroom with him. You were the only one who knew he sang to himself in the mirror every day. You promised never to tell another person about his singing, and he agreed to pay you ten dollars for your loyalty. You never told him, but you actually enjoyed his singing. You believed he would go on to become famous. Now that dream is shattered.

There were the times when you couldn't stand your sister. You were jealous of the attention your parents gave her over her good grades. You tried to get good grades, too, but never seemed to match her talents. There were the times when she was given an opportunity and you were left out. You didn't like having to share your bedroom with her. She always seemed to be bossy, and you just wanted her to leave you alone. Now she's gone, and you wish she were here to boss you around.

The relationship that brothers and sisters share is expected to be the longest relationship humans will ever have. It is a connection with someone who you assume will always be a part of your life. Brothers and sisters aren't supposed to die—not while they're young.

A family relationship between siblings is one of the most unique that you will ever encounter, simply because brothers and sisters are in our lives from the beginning. It is anticipated that they will be with us for our entire lives.

Throughout the twenty-first century, we have successfully conquered many childhood illnesses. Generally, children are living longer, and death during infancy is much less common. In spite of society's efforts, however, the current death rate for teenagers is growing. Young children and teenagers are dying as a result of violence, AIDS, suicide, and risk-taking behaviors, such as drugs or alcohol.

You may be reading this book because you or someone you care about has lost a sibling. This book was written to help offer support as you recover from the great pain of death. And although it might not seem like you will make it through the most difficult times, you can. You will feel happiness again.

Teenage years are filled with vigor and a strong belief in immortality. These challenging years are a time of finding meaning in life. They are a time when you test and protest all that you have been taught. Often, adolescents are filled with uncertainty and emotional turmoil, and facing the death of your brother or sister now is especially challenging. The loss of your sibling may at times make you feel as if you have lost a part of yourself, and yet, you will eventually find that you are able to go on living a complete life.

The information in this book will not always match your own experience. There are many ways that we suffer the painful process of grieving. Grieving is a human response to the loss of someone we love. As humans, we are all individuals. We each have different responses to nearly everything. Your brother or sister was as unique as your relationship with him or her. Now, your period of mourning will be a unique testament to the special relationship that you shared.

This Cannot Be Happening to Me

After the death of someone you love, you will experience intense emotions unlike any that you have felt before. This is part of the grieving process. Humans grieve when someone with whom they have formed a bond is no longer with them. There is no magical cure for the pain and distress that you will encounter while grieving. However, you will one day live again with much less pain.

Moving through grief can be considered a job. It is a job for which you did not apply; it was given to you. Your first task in this job that you did not seek is learning of the death. Your next task is to experience the deep pain and allow yourself to feel the many emotions that will arise. Another task is accepting the death of your brother or sister and continuing to enjoy your own life without that person's physical presence.

There is no exact formula or set amount of time for grieving. And although your grieving is unique, you are not alone. There are others who have hurt as you do now.

Time will ease your suffering. When legendary Tejano singer Selena Quintanilla Perez died, a family friend told Selena's sister, Suzette, that time would heal her sadness.

Suzette thought the friend was inconsiderate. Now, years later, she can affirm that time has eased her pain.

Shock

When you first receive the news of your brother's or sister's death, you may go into a state of shock. Your body begins to go on automatic pilot. You feel numb. For many, this is an initial reaction. For others, it may last for an extended period of time. Shock is a normal response. It may occur and reoccur at any time.

Shock, or emotional numbness, is nature's way of allowing your body time to cope with a tragic event. Your body moves slower as all of your systems slow down. Your heartbeat slows, breathing becomes shallow, and your blood pressure drops. Shock is a protective state. It allows us to begin preparing for the intense emotional and physical reactions that will follow.

Your brain functions may also slow down during this period. While your body is in shock, you may not hear people speaking to you. Very simple tasks become more laborious. It can be difficult to make decisions. The slowing down of your brain protects you from the over-load of pain. This time of shock can also allow you to accomplish necessary tasks.

For some people, the state of shock is so intense that they go into a state of denial. Sometimes, doing simple tasks such as helping to arrange a funeral may help those experiencing symptoms of denial.

Many teenagers report that their sense of shock lasted throughout the funeral until they were able to see the body of their sibling. Occasionally, even viewing the body does not reduce this state of numbness. Afterward, people who are still experiencing shock find that they remember little to nothing about the funeral service.

Armando

> *After my brother died, I became the oldest child. I didn't feel anything. I didn't even cry. I wondered if I was normal. I had no emotions for the entire first week. My parents needed a lot of help with things. I did what I was supposed to do without any emotion. Everyone thought I was strong. I guess I liked that people thought I was handling it so well.*

Armando finally began to experience the painful emotions of loss at his brother's graveside. After most of the guests had left, he felt a sudden rush of pain and lay across the casket. He cried there for more than twenty minutes. He knows today that his initial reaction was shock and that it enabled him to assist his parents. Later, Armando broke down many times and cried over the loss of his brother.

For many, the time of shock happens when family and friends are gathering together to support and honor the deceased. You may find that you don't want to talk to anyone. This is normal. You may keep yourself busy during this time with all the commotion, even if you feel lost.

Soon, the shock will wear away and the pain of human grief will remain. This may happen within a few hours of the death or a few days. For some, it may not happen for weeks.

Denial and Disbelief

Denial is a normal way in which humans adjust to a tragedy. Denial, like shock, is a mechanism that acts as a valve to enable us to tolerate small doses of a painful experience. It is sometimes the first reaction we have to the news of a death. Denial can also take the form of disbelief. As one student said, "I can't believe she is dead. We were just eating breakfast together this morning, and tomorrow we were going to go shopping for our prom dresses. She can't be dead. She has to be at graduation." Denying the reality of your loss should not become your way of dealing with pain.

Justin

"Where's my brother? He's here someplace, I know it. He just is. I know it! He's hiding under the bed like he always does." I called for Tommy again and again. I searched each of Tommy's favorite hiding places, but my three-year-old brother was not to be found.

Earlier that day, I had been called into the counselor's office at school, where I learned that Tommy had been rushed to the hospital after falling into a neighbor's swimming pool.

The counselor explained to me that Tommy had died at the hospital. He offered to drive me there to be with my parents, but I declined. I asked the counselor if he had any new scholarship forms. Then I thanked him for his time and returned to class.

I spent the rest of the day at school attending classes. I laughed with my friends at lunch and *planned to see them at the football game later that night. I did not tell anyone of my brother's death. I did not allow myself to think about it. I went through the day as though I had not received the startling news.*

I casually left school that afternoon with my best friend. When we arrived at my house, I insisted my friend not come in with me. Once inside, I tore through the house looking for my brother. When I couldn't find him, I banged my fists on the floor and screamed, "No, not my little brother, not Tommy!"

Justin's initial response to his brother's death was denial. This reaction enabled him to get through his day at school. It also allowed his mind and body some time to prepare to face the painful reality that awaited him. Only when he got home on the afternoon of Tommy's death did he begin to experience intense emotional pain.

Teenagers are especially likely to experience denial and disbelief when someone close to them has died. Some teenagers are able to control themselves and their emotions so well through denial or disbelief that others think they are well adjusted or even happy. In some cases, teenagers are thought of as uncaring because they are able to hide their pain. Shock, denial, and disbelief can also bring out emotional responses that may not seem appropriate. One thirteen-year-old boy even laughed when he first heard that his twin brother had been killed in an auto accident.

David

Late one August night, the phone rang at my home in Tucson. My father answered. It was Robert, my sister's boyfriend. He was going on about how the doctors had tried, but they just couldn't save Kim. It was hard to understand him because he was so upset. My father asked him to calm down and tell him what he meant. I hung up the other line; I didn't want to hear any more. I went back to my room and listened to my mother crying as my father told her Kim had died in an auto accident.

The next morning, my parents were talking about their plans to travel to Los Angeles. I insisted that the phone call was a joke. Kim could not really be dead. I remember feeling completely numb, virtually without any emotions.

Even though I didn't want to believe she had died, I flew with my family to Los Angeles. At the funeral, I watched as others cried and mourned my sister's death. At her graveside, I still felt nothing. I believed that if she was really dead, I would be crying like the others. I felt detached, as though I was watching it all happen.

David quickly returned to his regular routine, wondering if he was normal since he hadn't cried. It wasn't until he went into the darkroom in the photo lab at school that he was able to allow himself to feel the pain of his sister's death. Often, he cried in the darkroom during his senior year. He had found a place where he could allow himself to feel pain and finally cleanse his soul through his tears.

David's initial reaction was one of denial and disbelief. Shock, denial, and disbelief are nature's ways of allowing us time to come to accept the finality of death and gradually ease into the pain of our loss. Denial is a method that some people will use to block the pain of death for long periods of time. This will not work. Eventually, we all must face the intense emotional suffering of grieving for our loved one.

Denial and disbelief, like shock, can occur at any time in the grieving process. You may find yourself planning to pick up your brother after school and then remembering he isn't there anymore. It is natural to want to shut away events that are so painful. At times, your brain will give you confusing messages. You may even believe that you see your brother or sister lying in his or her bed. It will take some time for your brain to fully accept the reality of your sibling's death.

Loss Is Confusing and Painful

Upon learning of the death of your sibling, you may find that you are very confused. It may be difficult for you to accomplish simple tasks. Suddenly your world is forever changed. It is normal to be in a state of confusion. Your mind is taking the time that it needs to adjust.

The painful process of grieving will seem unbearable. You will find yourself overwhelmed with grief and sorrow unlike any you have ever experienced. This pain can be so great that you may begin to feel as though it's all a bad dream. You may be tempted to run from your pain or avoid feeling your grief by using substances that disengage your mind from reality. This is not a solution. Eventually, you will have to face your sorrow.

It is important that you allow yourself to feel grief. Since there is no correct method to the mourning process, there are no right or wrong feelings. Your emotions will be as unique as your personality. Others, even those close to you, may have very different feelings. Your grieving may take more or less time than the grieving of others. As you move through the pain, you will begin the process of healing.

As you begin to accept the reality of your sibling's death, you may experience a deep emptiness that feels like lead at the bottom of your stomach. You will yearn for someone or something to fill that empty void inside of you.

This is the beginning of your journey to find meaning and value in your life without a physical relationship with your deceased sibling. As you yearn for his or her physical presence, you will begin to find ways of remembering your sibling while continuing to live your life.

It Aches So Much

At times, the variety of emotions that you experience while grieving may cause you to withdraw from your normal routine. Grieving requires considerable energy, so it is normal to take some time off from activities.

Common emotions that most people experience when they lose someone they love are sadness and anger. You may find that you experience them at different levels and at different times. You may experience more than one emotion at a time or have mixed feelings like fear and guilt or relief and regret. What you feel will be as unique as you are.

As you begin to feel the pain of loss, you may find some of these activities helpful:

⇝ Writing about your feelings in a journal

⇝ Using some form of art, such as painting or drawing, to express your feelings

⇝ Talking about your emotions with a friend or adult

⇝ Listening to music

⇝ Exercising

⇒ Dancing as an expression of your feelings

⇒ Creating a video as a testament to your sibling's place within your family

⇒ Reading

⇒ Making a scrapbook

⇒ Planting a tree or garden

⇒ Getting involved in your community

⇒ Joining a support group

⇒ Making a banner or program to display at the funeral

⇒ Planing a Web site to honor your sibling

Sadness

Everyone experiences times when they are overwhelmed with sadness. Often you might feel like crying. This is a part of the human grieving experience that you should allow yourself. If you don't want others to see your tears, you may choose to be excused. Find a private area to let yourself go. Allow your tears to flow freely. You may prefer to wait until you are at home to cry. Tears are a natural part of the healing process; they allow a release of bodily toxins and provide a path toward soul cleansing.

Kara
I tried to go back to school the day after my sister's funeral. I believed it would be good to go back into my normal environment. While walking down the

hallway to class, I passed her locker. I couldn't take it. I started to feel tears in my eyes and ran into the bathroom. I stayed and cried by myself. I was too upset to return to my classes. Instead, I returned home and remained in my room for the rest of the day.

You could be enjoying moments with your friends and suddenly feel an overwhelming sadness. This feeling of depression may come up at any time and is a part of losing someone who was close to you. There is no abnormal amount of sadness. It will most likely be much stronger and more intense closer to the time of your loss, but it may come up many months and even years afterward.

Certain situations, obvious or not, may trigger your sadness. Normal daily activities that are filled with memories of your sibling can trigger your sadness at any time. There is no way to prepare for these experiences, so it is best to accept them whenever they present themselves.

Javier
My little sister loved to play with her stuffed animals, setting them up in front of the television. Sometimes, I teased her because she played with them. After she died, I couldn't stand to see commercials for little girls' toys. It would make tears come to my eyes. Now I feel guilty for my teasing. Mostly, I feel sad that she is gone.

Anger

Emily
Two weeks after my sister died, I felt like I was going to explode. I wanted to scream at everyone. One day

14

I yelled at my best friend for no reason. I was scared because I am usually very calm. My friend was very understanding. She let me cry.

Emily's anger was a surprise to her, and she wasn't certain how she should deal with it. Luckily, she had a very close friend who was there for her during her time of distress.

Anger is a very powerful emotion. It is also an emotion that we do not like to encounter because it can sometimes lead to extremely destructive behavior. It is best if you recognize your anger as normal and accept it. You may be angry at the world, at yourself, at your parents, and at the doctors for not saving your brother or sister. You may even be angry with your brother or sister for leaving you.

You may feel like lashing out, but it is natural to feel out of control. It is not okay to hurt yourself or others. There are safer ways of expressing your anger. If you need to scream, find a place, such as your bedroom, a deserted parking lot, or a meadow, or bury your face in a pillow, and allow yourself to scream.

Anger can be released in many ways. Try a physical activity that may be done alone, such as dancing, walking, or running. If you have a favorite sport, get involved in it. You may want to create some type of punching bag that you can hit. Some people find that involvement in the creative arts is a good place to release their anger. Great painters, such as Picasso, created amazing paintings out of their anger. Writing is another form of releasing your anger. Each person needs to discover safe methods of expressing anger and learn not to hurt himself or herself or others. Now is the time to develop your own methods for safely releasing anger.

Guilt

Many times, surviving brothers and sisters will experience a sense of guilt after their loss, feeling that they should also be dead. Occasionally, they feel responsible for the death of their sibling. If you feel guilt about your sibling's death, choose an adult friend or family member with whom you feel comfortable and discuss your feelings. Guilt is like a trap: If you aren't released from it, guilt will keep you in your state of pain. A caring person can listen to your feelings and help you find your way out of that trap.

Understanding death is like understanding that we are powerless to control our lives. To most people, this realization is initially paralyzing. To cope with our losses, and to cope with the understanding that we are indeed powerless, we sometimes embrace feelings of guilt instead. Guilt is an act of purposefully placing blame.

It is impossible to magically restore the past. You cannot go back in time to undo every wrong thing that you said or change anything that you may have done. Everyone experiences levels of guilt after a death. Perhaps you think you should have gone to the hospital, to the funeral, or to the gravesite. Maybe you remember moments when you could have been more understanding and sympathetic to your brother or sister. Whatever your regrets, it is important that you understand that you may very well be overly critical of your actions now. Talk about your feelings with other family members to help you gain some perspective.

Paul
   After the basketball game, my older brother, Jake, and I were out with friends one night having fun, as

always. It was the middle of the season. We weren't even drinking; that's not to say we don't drink, but it was the season and our coach made it clear we weren't allowed to drink. I hated always being the younger brother and sitting in the back of the car. That night, my brother let me sit up front and he sat in back. We were making a left turn when a pickup truck hit us. The driver and I were okay, but my brother was killed.

I was only a sophomore when Jake was a senior, and I felt lucky to be a part of the team. He was first string, point guard. After he died, I couldn't even think about playing anymore. I felt so guilty that he was dead. I felt that I didn't have the right to play; I shouldn't even be alive. I felt that I should have been the one who died; I should have been in the backseat.

The coach and team were at my brother's funeral. They were supportive. My coach let me sit out a few games, and then one day he asked me to play. I told him I couldn't. He understood. He told me that when I felt ready, I could play again. I think his understanding was what helped me. I didn't play that season, but I did play the following year. I still feel guilty sometimes, but now I figure I'll go on and win a game for Jake.

Paul's coach understood the pain that Paul was feeling. With the coach's help, he understood that he wasn't responsible for Jake's death. He was able to keep his brother in his life through playing a sport that they both loved.

Sometimes, people will believe they could have prevented the death of someone they love. They believe that if only they had done something different, then that person wouldn't have died. Accepting that we have no power or control over death is very frightening.

It is frightening to accept that we are powerless. It feels safer to feel guilty and to assign blame than to face our own powerlessness. Death is not preventable. Death is a reality that we will all face. You are not responsible for your brother's or sister's death.

You may have fought with your brother or sister. In fact, there were probably times when you couldn't stand him or her. Now that you have lost your sibling, you may feel guilty for not having been more loving. Remember, though, that your relationship with your brother or sister was one in which you shared closeness. And although your closeness may have been filled with arguments, you shared an intense intimacy that you did not share with others. That same intimacy and intensity may now bring you intense pain.

Envy

Sara

> *I started to cry one morning when I saw my parents leave for the cemetery together. "It just isn't fair that they still have each other and I don't have my sister anymore," I sighed.*

You may find yourself feeling jealousy toward your brother or sister who has died. It is common for people to glorify the dead person, often thinking only of the positive aspects of that person. Your parents may make comments that praise your sibling. Sometimes, this may cause you to feel that you aren't good enough. Remember, nobody is, or was, perfect.

Loneliness

Amber

> *I used to go to the mall with my sister to shop or just to hang around. We always had a great time. It's just not the same without her. She gave me advice on my clothing, and we flirted with guys and laughed at each other's jokes. Whitney wasn't just my sister. We were friends who did everything together.*

Amber felt very lonely after her sister died. Your sibling may have been a big part of your life, and now that he or she is gone, you may experience feeling alone for the first time.

Your brother or sister can never be replaced, and that makes it more difficult to tolerate loneliness. Often, humans will reach for someone to replace the person they have lost. This fulfillment is sometimes found in sexual intimacy. It is normal to want to feel close to someone when you are lonely.

Sexual intimacy can be a very loving and giving experience, but it cannot replace the person you have lost and it cannot take away your pain. Sometimes, people believe that sexual intimacy will provide temporary relief from suffering. You must be extremely cautious when considering an intimate relationship shortly after the loss of a loved one. If you need emotional closeness and your partner's needs are only physical, it could cause you further pain.

Shortly after the death of a loved one, you may not be thinking clearly about safe sexual practices. Consider that there is the possibility of pregnancy and sexually transmitted diseases, or STDs. With as many emotions as you may be feeling, it may be a very inappropriate time to enter into any sexual relationship. The loneliness that you are feeling will eventually disappear.

Feelings of loneliness can even occur when you are with a group of people. You may feel as if no one around you really understands. Your family may be occupied with their own pain and unavailable to you. There may be other times when you prefer to be alone. Being alone isn't the same as feeling lonely. You may enjoy the peace and quiet that you find when you are by yourself.

Fear

Many fears may surface after you have experienced the death of someone who was close to you. You may become afraid of your own death or of losing a person that is close to you, such as a parent, teacher, or relative. Even though you are full of life like most teenagers, you are now faced with trying to understand mortality. Understanding death and mortality is terrifying for everyone.

Feeling fearful of your own death is normal and should not be repressed. Talking about your fears will help you overcome them. If your brother or sister died after a long illness, you may fear that you have the same or another illness. This sort of "identification" illness has been seen in many case studies of persons who are working through the grief process. For example, if your brother died of a heart condition, you may actually feel yourself having chest pains, or if your sister died of pneumonia, you may sense that you are feeling feverish. If you do feel any unusual physical symptoms, however, you should speak with your doctor.

Ambivalence

The death of your brother or sister may bring about some confusing feelings and thoughts. You may feel fortunate that it wasn't you who died. This, too, is a normal feeling. Adolescence is a time filled with a great deal of uncertainty. It is also a time when humans become aware of the existence of a life beyond their immediate experience. The death of someone close to you may cause you to feel frightened about your own future.

Relief

Tyler

My brother had leukemia and had been sick for a long time. Sometimes, when he was in pain, I would just pray and ask God to take him. I hated to see him hurting so much. It was sad to watch him become more and more sickly. I felt bad that I wanted him to die, but I wanted his suffering to end.

Tyler's deep level of caring caused him to wish his brother's suffering would stop. He knew that death was the only solution. If your sibling has been sick for a long time, you may feel relieved that his or her suffering has stopped, or that your own prolonged period of living with someone who required caregiving is over. It is sometimes very oppressive to have a family member who is sick and dying. Maybe you were responsible for caring for your brother or sister and now you have the freedom to do other, more personal, activities, such as spending time with friends. Feeling a sense of relief after the death is very normal.

21

Regret

Regret is a common emotion after a loved one's death because every family shares arguments and bad feelings at one time or another. It is also very common for siblings to have disagreements. You may wish you could take back all the fighting and unkind words. You may regret the time that you won't have with your sibling and your plans that won't happen. Indeed, your life will be very different without that person's presence.

Kyle
> *My brother and I fought all the time. It seemed like we never got along. Now, I wish things had been different. I see other brothers together, and I think that if Joseph were still here, I wouldn't worry about all the stuff that used to bother me. I would spend more time with him.*

Kyle regretted the many difficult times he had with his brother. Regrets are a normal part of grieving. Relationships are filled with good times and bad. Your relationship with your brother or sister was what it was meant to be. Those instances in which you treated your brother or sister in ways you now regret were a part of what made your relationship unique.

Embarrassment

As a teenager, you want to fit in. You want to be a part of a group. Experiencing peer pressure sometimes means not wanting to be different from members of that group. The death of your sibling has made you different, and you may, at times, feel some embarrassment from it. You may even feel bad about your embarrassment. This, too, is a natural part of reacting to your experience with death.

Grieving is part of losing someone we love. It won't last forever. With time, you will begin to feel better. The process of grieving is very tiresome. Sometimes, you'll need a break from your pain. It is okay to allow yourself time to enjoy life. When you are in the mood, enjoy the activities that make you happy. You don't have to remain sad all the time.

People may think that they are "going out of their minds" when they are grieving. You may find that you aren't able to concentrate on even the simplest tasks. You may also find that there are times when you can't stop thinking about your deceased sibling. Perhaps you feel like you will just burst wide open and say or do things that you normally wouldn't.

With so many intense emotions racing through you, it's no wonder you may feel as though you are going crazy. What you are experiencing is common. Many people who have lost someone they love begin to feel as though they are losing their minds. If you find that you are becoming overwhelmed, search for methods to release your frustrations that are not destructive to yourself or others.

Eddie

Everywhere I looked I saw the image of my brother's face. I saw his reflection on billboards and on walls. Once, while walking alone, I saw his face on the sidewalk. I couldn't take it anymore. Suddenly, I started to cry.

23

When I stopped walking, I noticed people had been staring at me. Someone came up and asked me if I was okay. I felt kind of embarrassed. But then I realized that I felt a little better. I gained a lot from this emotional release. I wasn't lost in my emotions anymore.

If you need an adult to talk to for support, try some of these people:

⮑ Parents, aunts, uncles, and grandparents

⮑ Teachers, scout leaders, and coaches

⮑ Ministers, rabbis, and priests

⮑ Doctors, nurses, and social workers

⮑ Counselors and mentors

I Think I'm
Going Crazy

The inability to concentrate on activities is also a normal part of the grieving process. It is understandable if your mind is absorbed with thoughts of your deceased sibling. Your mind is also very busy with all kinds of emotions, and, at times, you may need to just sit back and let yourself relax. If you can, take a nap or go for a walk. Try to give yourself periodic breaks from the strong emotional concentration that grips you.

Ruben

It had been two months since my brother died, and I was still thinking of him every day. Like the time when I was playing soccer and Frank's face kept appearing in my mind. I couldn't think of anything else; I had to sit down. My friends were okay with my behavior. They understood.

During geometry class, I couldn't concentrate. Finally, my geometry teacher told me that I had been distracted long enough. She wanted me to start paying attention. I was hurt. I tried, but I couldn't get my brother out of my mind. I didn't do very well in geometry. In fact, I failed most of my classes that year.

Unexplained Experiences

Christina

I was sixteen when my sister, Lillian, died. She was twelve years old and had just started middle school. I clearly remember the night before her first day of school because she kept asking me questions. She wouldn't let me sleep. Sometimes, as I was falling asleep, she would start singing her favorite songs. I would get so mad at her. I just wanted her to quiet down and go to sleep.

I miss her now. The first night after she died, I just kept looking over at her empty bed, crying. I had to sleep in another room. After the funeral, I started to sleep in my room again. I lay in my bed, and I heard her singing. I know people don't believe me, but I did. She was singing. At first, it scared me. I went to another room to sleep.

I tried sleeping in my room again the next night. Just as I was falling asleep, she started to sing. It scared me, but when I listened, I felt this peace inside me. The following night was the same; I still heard her singing. She sang every night for three weeks. The first night that she didn't sing, I missed it. Sometimes she still sings for me, like when I am upset.

I know it sounds crazy, and I don't like to tell many people because they don't believe me. I feel like she's still with me.

Many people who have lost someone close to them report hearing and seeing things that they just can't explain. These urgent feelings of unreality are called hallucinations and may make you feel as if you are experiencing sights, sounds, or impressions of unreal experiences. This does not mean you are insane. Most psychiatrists have noted that a preoccupation with the deceased individual is common. In fact, the idea of temporary hallucinations is so common that a disassociation with reality is considered a part of the grief process, or grief work. If you find the experiences to be very disturbing, you may want to consult with a professional, such as your family doctor or a grief therapist.

It is normal to want to keep your brother or sister close to you in some form. He or she may have left you physically, but he or she did not leave your heart and soul. One young man found that wearing his brother's clothing kept him close to his sibling whom he loved and admired.

Panic

You may find yourself suddenly fearful about the smallest things. You may panic when you can't find your shoes. You may be panicking over your own future and what your brother's or sister's death means for you. Making decisions can become very difficult. This is all perfectly normal. However, you may want to put off making important decisions until you are feeling more confident.

Physical Reactions

Even your body may respond to the death of your sibling with some symptoms, but not everyone has physical responses. Here are some of the most common:

Sleeping: You may sleep more or less than usual. Some people have nightmares. If you are having difficulty sleeping, try reading a book, listening to comforting

27

music, or drinking hot, decaffeinated tea or warm milk before going to bed. Some people find that sleep is the only time they are able to get some peace.

Tightness: You may experience tightness in your chest or throat. Or you might experience a shortness of breath or sensations that simulate those of being choked. If any of these experiences happen to you, it is important to seek help from an adult, preferably a medical professional.

Fatigue: Grieving is very tiring. You may feel exhausted more often than is usual for you. Feelings of exhaustion are somewhat universal among those who are experiencing grief. You may find that you are unable to climb stairs or that walking any distance is nearly impossible. Now is the time to rest. Allow your body to determine your pace.

Hyperactivity: Some people respond to a death by seeming to have extra energy; they simply can't sit still. These spurts of energy, or hyperactivity, may make you feel great restlessness. Some people walk around aimlessly or find that they search for tasks to complete to help keep busy. While there is nothing wrong with helping family during a trying time, don't avoid feeling the emotions that are welling inside your mind. Releasing emotion is the beginning of the healing process.

Eating: Eating habits may change while you are grieving. Just like sleeping, some people find that they eat more, or less, as a way of dealing with their stress. It is very normal for your body to be disinterested in eating while you are grieving. Even though you may not feel like eating, it is important that you maintain a minimal intake of food and water. Your body needs energy and nourishment to survive. If you are eating more than usual, be sure that you are not using food as a way to avoid your feelings. If you are at all concerned about any physical changes in your body or any other problems, you should seek medical advice from your doctor.

Depression

You may be feeling like there isn't anything good or happy left in the world since your brother or sister died. There may be times when you don't want to do anything or see anyone. You may have doubts about the meaning of life and its value. These kinds of feelings are symptoms of depression.

Depression is a very common reaction to the loss of a loved one. Some people find they don't want to go on with their own lives. It is important to remember that there is no way of bringing back your brother or sister. While it is acceptable to feel depressed and to wonder about the value of living, it is important that you do not act on these feelings and hurt yourself.

If you begin to have thoughts or feelings about ending your own life, speak with someone immediately. Your own self-destruction will not change your loss. You are an individual with your own life to live. At this point, your road is very painful. It is important to recognize that these destructive thoughts are only temporary.

Recognize the Signs of Depression

- Altered sleep patterns, either excessive or resulting in insomnia
- Prolonged withdrawal from friends and activities
- Deterioration of relationships
- Engaging in risk-taking behaviors like abusing drugs and alcohol
- Inability to experience pleasure
- Feeling overly guilty, angry, hostile, or resentful
- Feeling helpless or hopeless for prolonged periods of time
- Radical appetite changes, eating too little or too much

If you are experiencing any combination of the warning signs listed above, it is very important that you seek the help of a professional doctor, psychiatrist, psychologist, grief therapist, social worker, schoolteacher, or any other adult mentor who can help guide you through this period in your life.

Because you are grieving deeply, this may be the first time when you have felt no inspiration. Inspiration is there. One day you will feel it again and find a renewed pleasure in living.

Some people have used journals as places to record their feelings when they have lost someone they love. Joshua didn't want to do anything after his brother Raymond died.

He became very depressed. He stayed in his darkened room and didn't speak with anyone. His family became concerned. After four weeks, he returned to school.

Joshua

We had been keeping journals that year in our English class. The teacher always gave some directions for journal writing, and that day she told us to write a conversation that we wanted to have with someone. This person could be dead or alive, she said. I was ready to scream! How could she say this? Didn't she know about me?

I didn't scream. I wrote about telling my brother how much I loved him. I said I was sorry for the arguments that we had. I told him how much I loved it when he made me laugh. I told him about the time when he thought the neighbor had stolen his baseball glove when I was the one who lost it. I kept writing the entire period. I didn't even hear the bell ring.

For the rest of that year, I wrote in my journal about my brother and how much I missed him. Some days, I was hurting so much that the only thing I could do was write. I still have my journal today. That journal gave me a place to say anything I felt. Now I can see it and feel glad that I don't feel so bad anymore.

Will I Ever Be Normal Again?

After the initial denial and disbelief wore away, Justin began to feel the tremendous pain of losing his brother. He had friends who were there for him when he needed them, and he had returned to his life filled with school, the drama club, his job, and soccer.

Justin

It had been just about a year and a half since Tommy had drowned. I went out with my friends one night. It was spring break, and I was feeling great. We did all of our usual stuff. It was almost as though nothing had happened.

Then, the next morning, I woke up with this sick feeling in my stomach. I felt so empty and alone. I wanted to scream and yell. I was still very angry and frustrated that my brother was gone. The pain was so intense. It was nearly too much to take.

I ran over to the neighbor's pool where Tommy had drowned. I jumped in with all my clothes on. I went crazy, screaming, "Tommy! Tommy!" I dove down to the bottom of the pool trying to find him. I guess my father had been watching me. He was at the side of the pool when I got out. He hugged me, and we stood there crying together.

I thought I was over the pain, but it returned so suddenly. I was thankful that my father was there because I knew I wasn't the only one still hurting.

You may find times when you think you are feeling better, and then, just like Justin, you are suddenly overwhelmed with turmoil. This is a part of losing someone you love. The pain may return many months after the death. You will still experience moments when you will be both overwhelmed and confused. These emotions will soon pass.

How to Contain Intense Emotions

When you experience intense emotional turmoil, you should find a safe manner of releasing and expressing yourself. There are ways of finding relief from this type of emotional intensity. You may need a place, like a container of sorts, to store your emotions. You can create your own "storage facility" for your pain. For example, think of the storage centers where people store things that they aren't using.

One young woman found her sketches were a place to store her emotions. She created several drawings, which were reflections of the feelings she had over the loss of her little brother. One young man who didn't like to write decided to tape-record all of his thoughts and feelings. The cassette then became a container holding his pain. Perhaps you have a favorite spot where you could go and deposit your pain. This is another form of a container for intense emotions.

It is okay to feel strong emotions, but you must not be destructive with those feelings. Grieving cannot be escaped. Some people attempt to escape the pain with drugs and alcohol, but using substances will not take the pain away.

For a long time after the loss of a sibling, you may feel vulnerable. There will be times when you will regress to immature actions. It is very normal to feel like you want someone to care for you. Feeling vulnerable can be very frightening. Sometimes, because we are in pain, we act strongly with others when we feel most in need of their care. We are afraid they will cause us further pain. This tough attitude can sometimes drive people away when we need them most. If there is someone you trust, it is okay to accept his or her help.

Comforting Yourself

It is not always possible to have someone comfort and care for you in the ways that you crave. You will need to find methods of comforting yourself that can bring you feelings of security.

It is important that you select methods of self-comforting that are not destructive to yourself or others. Some teenagers have found that listening to certain types of music is reassuring. You may find that the style of music you normally listen to does little to provide you with the comfort you need. Explore musical styles and allow yourself to accept that you may find comfort from a different, and maybe even unexpected, style of music. You may seek comfort in a familiar book, in sleeping, or spending time with friends or animals.

Illegal drugs, alcohol, and sexual intimacy are all methods that some people use to comfort themselves. These methods do bring a temporary reprieve from painful experiences. But there is a price to pay when we choose these methods of comfort. You could become dependent on an addictive substance, or you could end up pregnant, with an STD, or in an unhealthy relationship.

Abusing drugs, drinking alcohol, and using sexual relations as sources of comfort will not bring the lasting solace and easing of your pain that you seek. You cannot escape your pain. These actions may help you avoid dealing with your pain on the surface, but your pain is still inside of you. If you abuse drugs or use sex to keep yourself from experiencing anguish, you will continue to suffer.

When we lose someone we love, we find ourselves feeling as though we have no control over the events in our lives. As a teenager, your days are filled with insecurity. The loss of a brother or sister may make you feel even more insecure. When we are very young, we often cling to an object for comfort. This method may still be effective. You may find that an item of your brother's or sister's, such as a favorite sweatshirt, pajamas, or sweater, is comforting to keep close to you. This is a very normal method of helping to console yourself as well as keeping the memory of your sibling close.

The advice in this book may not be enough for you. You may find you need to seek some outside help. There are many trained professionals who can assist you. The next chapter will give you some direction toward finding those who can and will help you make it through your loss.

Am I Alone? Does Anyone Care?

You have just lost your brother or sister, and you find yourself wanting to be with people. You want people to help; you want them to hold you and offer support. You may want them to remove all of your pain. Unfortunately, no one can take away that pain. Some people may be able to offer you comfort, while others may be able to distract you from your pain.

Occasionally, people will tell you to get on with life even though you can see only darkness. Most people who make these comments do so because they are unable to tolerate sadness. They want to see you happy. They don't understand that you need time to be sad. Others may tell you that you should be feeling better when you are still hurting. There are no "shoulds" in human grieving.

You may also find that when someone offers help and support, you react with anger and reject help. You have just suffered a great loss, and you may not be able to trust others. It is normal to be distrustful when you are hurting. Like a wounded animal, you are protecting yourself. There are those whom you can trust. You will slowly learn who can and will offer you their compassion and support.

Helpful Friends

April

> *I was at my friend Cindy's house when I learned that my brother had passed away. He had been sick for two years, and we knew he was going to die. My friend's mother told me that my mother was on the phone. I knew that it was bad news. My mother told me that Jack had died.*
>
> *I was in shock. Even though we knew he was going to die, it still hit me hard. I fell into a chair and couldn't say anything. My friend told my mother that she shouldn't worry—she would take care of me. I don't remember because I was just so removed. My friend helped me walk to the couch to rest. She sat near me and stroked my hair while I just lay staring at the ceiling. After a while I was able to tell her that I wanted to go home. She stayed with my family. I was glad she did. Everyone was so busy with the preparations. With Cindy by my side, though, I didn't feel so alone. She was able to be with me during the funeral. In fact, she was there for me throughout the entire first year after Jack's death. She was always there for me.*

Hurtful Remarks

Some of your family and friends may treat you differently after your sibling's death, since the topic of death and loss make many people very uncomfortable. They don't know what to say or do for the living relatives and friends of the one who has died. They feel uncomfortable with the topic because it causes them to fear their own death. This can make it more difficult for you.

Listen carefully for remarks like "I understand how you feel," "Your sibling led a full life," "You must be strong," "Don't cry," or "It was the will of God." These remarks are counterproductive because they are "closed." Closed remarks do not lead to an open discussion of how you are feeling and are not productive for emotional healing.

It is normal to want to have people around you to help you feel less alone. Many remarks that people make when someone has died are hurtful, causing less comfort than harm. Most people don't intentionally say hurtful things to someone who has just lost a relative, but occasionally even well-intentioned comments can leave a person feeling emptier and more confused.

Anthony
Even though my friends tried to make me feel better, sometimes they said things that made me feel worse. For instance, one friend said my brother's death was "God's way" and that I should just accept it. Some of the guys tried to tell me that it was for the best. I know they meant well, but I was really hurting and didn't believe that. Mostly, though, it was good to have friends. They helped me when I wanted to get my mind off my brother's accident.

Anthony found that his friends did not always say what he wanted to hear, but they were his friends. They helped provide him with the company he needed during a lonely time in his life.

Your friends may feel awkward around you. It is okay to let them know how you are feeling and what you would like for them to do for you. Your friends may be good people with whom you can share your feelings about your sibling's death.

People who are grieving are desperate to find comfort in the company of others and seek relief from their loneliness through contact with others. In desperation, some are even willing to allow people to say and do things that hurt them without speaking up. While you are grieving, it is acceptable to let others know when they have offended you. It is okay to be selective about whom you wish to spend time with.

Nicole

I couldn't understand my boyfriend. After my baby sister died, he told me that it didn't matter much since I hadn't wanted my mother to have another baby. Sure, I wasn't very happy when she told me she was pregnant, but that didn't mean I wanted the baby to die. As it was, I was feeling guilty because I hadn't been too excited about Brenda being born. My boyfriend just made me feel worse. He thought I shouldn't be so upset. Finally, I couldn't be around him anymore because he would ignore me whenever I was sad.

I was becoming increasingly depressed and didn't know what to do. I was watching a television show where this woman was talking about her baby who was born dead. Even though she hadn't wanted the child, she was very upset when the doctor told her that her baby was stillborn. She said that she felt so guilty, like she had made the baby die by not wanting it. That was just how I was feeling.

At the end of the show, the host mentioned a telephone number that you could call if you wanted help. When I called, they gave me some names and numbers for counselors in my own city. I told my mother that I wanted to see a counselor. She was so relieved. I went for about three months. The therapist helped me understand that I didn't cause Brenda's death. She understood that I was sad even though I hadn't wanted another sister.

Support Networks

Support Groups

Many teenagers have found that support groups provide them with what they need after the death of someone they love. Support groups made up of teenagers who are grieving and a mediation counselor will give you a place to go and speak with others who are going through similar periods in their lives. A trained counselor leads the group, and there are certain rules that all participants are required to follow. One rule that is applied in all groups is a policy of privacy. The information that is shared in the group remains in the group. This gives each participant the freedom to say things that he or she might not want others outside the group to hear.

Chad

When my twin brother, Travis, died, I felt like he had taken a part of me with him. Travis and I were more than just brothers—we were best friends. I felt like I had lost two people. After the funeral, I went back to school and tried to be normal. It wasn't easy. I began to get into fights, and my grades were quickly dropping. My algebra teacher asked me to come in after school one day. He explained that he had lost his twin brother when he was eight years old. Then he told me about a support group for teenagers who are grieving.

I felt somewhat relieved after he had told me about his brother. I guess I didn't feel so alone. I started attending the group and found it was good for me. I was able to talk about my brother with other teenagers. Together, we shared our stories and our feelings. It has been three years since Travis died. I don't think I would have been able to cope without my teacher's help and the help of the support group.

Family

It is helpful if you are able to express your feelings to family members. This may not always be possible, though. Death is a time of hardship for families. Because your parents are caught up with their own suffering, they may be unable to give you the support that you need. Your other siblings may seem distant, and you may not understand each other's way of grieving.

Some families, though, have found that they are able to provide each other with added comfort after a death in the family. They may share comforting memories of the deceased. You may find that talking with your family is a great network of support.

41

Teachers and Other School Staff
Perhaps you have had a teacher who has been there for you in a special way in the past. This person may be a good resource for you now. School counselors have had training in helping teenagers to cope with some of their stress. Your school counselor may not be able to provide you with the specific help that you want, but he or she should be able to refer you to someone in the community who can assist you.

Spiritual Support
During your time of grief, you may need someone who can help you with questions about the nature of life and death. We have no real knowledge of what happens after death. The explanations for our state after we die are found in our individual spiritual beliefs and pursuits. Spiritual leaders are also prepared to help you deal with losses in your life. You may find that now would be a good time to speak with your pastor, priest, rabbi, or other spiritual leader.

Medical Professionals
Doctors and nurses can answer any questions that you may have about your sibling's death. They are also able to address any concerns you may have about your own health. If your sibling died from an illness, you may begin fearing that you will become ill. You may even begin to experience symptoms that are similar to those of the illness that struck your deceased sibling. It is important that you speak with your doctor about these feelings, especially if you are not feeling well. Your doctor can provide you with accurate information about your own health as well as the cause of death of your sibling.

Grief Therapists

Carrying the weight of losing a sibling can be a great burden, and a grief therapist is specifically trained to help people find their own coping methods.

Asking for help is not a sign of weakness. If you feel that you need someone to speak with, you can feel confident that there are caring therapists who will give you professional assistance during this painful time. If your loss feels overwhelming, you can find someone who will help you.

When you begin looking for help, there are several sources you may want to explore. Your family doctor may be able to refer you to a specialist, a school counselor can refer you to a social worker, or you may want to check in the yellow pages for a therapist. A family member may also be able to help you choose a counselor.

Carrying the heavy burden of losing a sibling is discomforting. We all have times when we need to lean on someone for support. Sometimes, though, family and friends aren't what we want or need them to be during our times of greatest need. Sometimes, even close friendships end when someone dies.

Accepting help from others is difficult and frustrating. While suffering with your loss, it may not be easy to trust others. You may say things to people that are hurtful. And although this behavior may drive them away, this is our method of protecting ourselves.

There are caring people who can be trusted to be there for you. You may find these people in your own social circles or you may not. It takes some effort, but if you are willing to look beyond your own immediate friends, you may find that caring individual.

Sacha

After a sibling dies, he or she will always remain with you. It was just like that when my sister Erin died. She and I were very close, and I found that the only person who truly understood my loss was a friend that I had made in school that same year, Sharon.

Sharon knew how I was feeling from the very beginning. One day, I shared my feelings with her about how close I had been with Erin. I explained how much Erin meant to me and how she was always so helpful, so involved in my life. Erin's death had been devastating. I felt like I was in a dark, inescapable tunnel. I couldn't concentrate. Erin had always been in my life, and now she was gone forever.

Like me, Sharon had lost her sister. And although her situation wasn't exactly like mine, she understood how important it had been to have an older sister guiding you through tough times. We laughed and cried about our experiences and what our sisters had tried to teach us about life. We both shared our painful memories and our regret.

Sharon completely understood my pain because she had experienced so much hardship during the long battle with her sister's illness before she died. Carla had succumbed to cancer just a few months earlier. Sharon explained that she felt fortunate to have had time to say good-bye. Sharon understood my anger. She also reassured me that the angry feelings would pass if I talked about how I'd been feeling.

Together we remembered how our families had been before these tragedies, and together we cried. I don't know what I would have done without Sharon's encouragement. We became nearly insepa-rable after that year. It was as though we had become sisters to each other.

Funerals Help Us Say Good-Bye

Throughout the ages, all cultures have held rituals for the dead to help friends and family cope with their grief. A funeral is a traditional ritual that allows family and friends to gather together to commemorate the life of the one who has died. Often the beginning of experiencing the deep process of mourning, a funeral helps the living accept the reality of death.

But the funeral needn't be filled with only sadness. Not everyone feels a funeral should be a somber event. A funeral is a time when family members who haven't seen each other for many years gather together. This sometimes leads to a festive affair. Some cultures use the funeral as a celebration—a last celebration for the person who has died. It is a time to remember all that the person was and the importance of that person's life.

Prior to the funeral, there are many tasks that need to be completed. Decisions regarding the funeral can be overwhelming. You may wish to be a part of that decision making or to help in the selections for the service. It is important that you make your wishes known. You may not be given the opportunity to make decisions, but if it is your desire, let your family know how you feel.

The amount of time between the death and the funeral is dependent on several factors. An autopsy may be required, and this will demand time. If the deceased was a murder victim, time will also be required for a thorough police investigation to help determine the culprit. Locating any clues that are pertinent to the police investigation is an important task that you and your family will want to see carried out properly. It is also necessary to have time to make the funeral arrangements and gather together.

An official from the clergy, such as a priest, rabbi, or minister, normally conducts funerals. However, this is not always the case. The person conducting the funeral may or may not have known the deceased. The family can provide that person with important information about their loved one, such as details about his or her life and the people and places he or she enjoyed. While families often make similar decisions about funerals, there are some differences that are dependent upon certain religious and cultural factors. In most cases, someone who knew the deceased will share thoughts about the person. There is also spiritual music and a time of silence as the attendees remember the deceased.

Because your sibling was special in your life, you may want to share some of your thoughts at the funeral. There may be others who knew and loved your sibling, too, and you may wish to hear them speak. Listening to words of praise from your sibling's friends may help to comfort you during your time of distress. Other family preparations prior to a funeral include making banners, photo collages, and, in some cases, programs filled with sentiments to honor the deceased. All of the preparation that becomes part of the funeral service will help your family share their love of the deceased and formally close a door on an important part of their life.

Like a funeral, a memorial service also commemorates the life and death of a person. With a memorial service, however, there is no burial. Memorial services are sometimes held instead of a funeral. People who knew and cared for the deceased may get together and plan an honorary tribute, an occasion where kind words and sentiments are expressed.

Some teenagers may not want to attend a funeral or memorial service because they are fearful. You will need to decide for yourself whether or not to attend.

Lisa

My sister was away at college when she died in an auto accident. My parents went to Ohio to arrange for her body to be sent home. We thought we would have a small, quiet funeral service. Laura hadn't had many friends in our town, and my parents were very private people. So we were very surprised when more than seventy-five college students drove 500 miles to attend Laura's funeral.

We hadn't realized she had so many friends. A couple of them asked if they could say a few words in honor of Laura at her funeral. My father was hesitant, but he let them speak. They talked about her outgoing and friendly attitude and her giving spirit. I am so glad they spoke. I realized that, while I loved my sister, I didn't know her. We were living in two different worlds. It was therapeutic to hear them talk about her positive traits.

48

Body Preparation

Embalming is a typical practice in America that exchanges blood and other body fluids from the dead body with artificial preservatives. This process helps to slow the body's decomposition. Although law does not require it, embalming has become almost a standard practice because it allows the body to be viewed during the funeral.

The family selects the clothing their loved one will be dressed in at the funeral. Some families select items that were important to the deceased, such as a favorite pair of jeans or sports jersey. Usually these items are a reflection of their loved one's life.

Cremation

Sometimes, people choose to be cremated instead of buried when they die. With cremation, the body is heated to a high temperature. Because the human body is made up of 90 percent water, at that temperature all of the body tissues evaporate. Remaining bone matter, called cremains, are crushed into a fine powder, or ashes, that are normally placed in a container called an urn. Some people ask that the ashes be spread over a place that was special to them, such as a favorite ocean or park. However, your family may choose to keep the urn in a special place of honor.

Entombment

In America, we have traditionally buried our dead in the ground, but now families can choose entombment. This choice is similar to a burial, but the body is kept above the ground in a mausoleum. Like a gravesite, the family can go and visit their loved one's mausoleum.

Viewing the Body

Many funerals in America have an open casket, allowing family and friends an opportunity to see the deceased one last time. For some, viewing the body is a time when they are able to fully accept the reality of their loved one's death.

Many funerals are preceded by a wake, often held at the funeral home. The wake is usually held the day or evening before the burial so that relatives and friends may pay their final respects to the deceased. The coffin may either be open or closed during this time, depending on the family's wishes. The wake often helps the family to prepare for the event of the next day's final burial.

Seeing a loved one as a corpse can be very painful and traumatic. Because you may not be able to handle this, the decision to view your brother's or sister's body should be made by you. You may be confused about your decision. If you need some support, you can talk with a member of the clergy, a family member, or the funeral director.

Maria

I watched as all my aunts touched and kissed my little sister's face and hands. They would hold her hand and then just start crying. I wanted to touch her, too, but I was scared. My grandmother came and walked with me to the casket. I rested my hand on her cheek. It felt hard, and then I knew she was dead. She didn't have any life in her. I started to cry just like my aunts.

Funerals Help Us Say Good-Bye

It was just so difficult to really believe that some-one so sweet, innocent, and happy could just die. She was a little girl, but now she was lifeless. It felt horrible to touch her dead body, but it gave me a chance to say good-bye.

Some people are afraid that if they see their loved one in the casket, they will never be able to picture that person in any other way. If you choose not to attend the funeral however, you may regret it, because you would have liked to say good-bye.

Shanel

My brother was seventeen when he died. He was on the city all-star football team. Everybody liked Aaron. He was a class clown and made everyone laugh. His teachers even liked him because he'd get everyone's attention.

The church was packed for my brother's funeral. My older brother Kevin stood and told some stories about Aaron, and everyone laughed. It was perfect because he liked to hear people laughing.

Things got more serious when the preacher spoke. We were quiet and respectful. Later, though, we began laughing and having a good time as we remembered Aaron. I think it was good that we didn't sit around and cry. We wanted to remember the Aaron we knew.

Funerals are most often a painful event. There may be unexpected behaviors from people during funerals and tense moments. It is an emotional event, and you may wit-ness relatives expressing their feelings in ways that you have not seen before. Not all families are intact and cooperative. Funerals can sometimes bring up old family issues. There may be family members at the funeral who make you feel uncomfortable. Getting through a funeral is a very painful and difficult challenge, even for adults.

Commemorating your brother or sister is an important aspect of the funeral. You may want to create other forms of expression that memorialize the life of your brother or sister. Here are a few suggestions that other teenagers have found beneficial:

- ↝ Write a poem, story, or song that is a reflection of your brother or sister.

- ↝ Create artwork, such as a sculpture, painting, collage, poster, or drawing.

- ↝ Dedicate music through the local radio station to your sibling.

- ↝ Put together a scrapbook in honor of your brother or sister.

- ↝ Finish a project that your brother or sister started.

- ↝ Create a Web page in honor of your sibling.

- ↝ Make a memorial to your sibling that your family can share.

Funeral preparations combined with visits from family or friends should help console you during the most painful time of your loss. The period of time just after the funeral is often very difficult because family and friends who were there for support have now returned to their lives.

Jewish Traditions

Because the time just after a funeral is so difficult, the ancient religion of Judaism holds a mourning ritual called a shivah. Lasting three to seven days, the shivah gathers friends and family together every night to celebrate the deceased by reading Hebrew prayers, telling stories, and enjoying family memories. Because of the family's respect for the deceased individual, they are usually discouraged from answering doors or phones during this time. They are also discouraged from cooking, cleaning, or doing any sort of work. After a shivah has ended, a rabbi may gather the immediate family for a brief neighborhood walk or a talk about returning to life's work.

No matter what your family's faith, you could conduct your own version of the shivah tradition. Gather family members together to announce your plans and then assign each member a task, such as searching for family albums, videos, favorite songs or poems, and passages from books. Take time to create a special, spiritual environment in your home that will allow everyone a chance to grieve both individually and as a family unit. By adopting this ancient tradition, you offer support to your family after the funeral is over as well as some peace of mind.

Life Goes On

The funeral is over, and now you are faced with the reality of continuing with your life. Unfortunately, it will never be as it was. Your task now is to return to your daily activities without your sibling. You have no choice. This task was assigned to you, and you must proceed.

Grieving takes time and energy. You may find that you aren't able to continue everything in your normal routine. This is okay. If you become overwhelmed as you attempt to accomplish everything you used to do, stop and prioritize your activities. Make a list of everything you normally do and decide which items on the list must be done and which can be ignored. One day you will be able to return to your full schedule.

Some people feel guilty when they begin to have fun after they have lost someone they love. It is good to put your mourning aside and enjoy yourself. Allow some time for activities that you enjoy, such as going to the movies or spending time with friends.

How Should I Tell People? Do I Have to Tell People?

The decision of whom to tell is your own. Some people find that they prefer to keep things to themselves as much as possible, while others like to have many people know they have lost someone. You may want to share only with people who you feel will be supportive of you.

Sometimes the people with whom you share may not respond in a helpful manner. And while many of your closest friends may be aware of your sibling's death, your teachers may not have any knowledge of your situation.

Returning to
Previous Routines

Angelica

One situation that was really difficult was encountering someone who hadn't heard about my sister's accident. A person might ask me if Jessica was planning to play basketball at college. Or someone else might ask me to say hello to my sister.

If I was upset at the time someone asked for her, I would break down and cry. Once, I became so angry when someone called for her that I screamed into the telephone. I told the person she should know my sister had died. Most of the time, people who didn't know were very kind when I told them. They would tell me they were sorry and then talk about what a wonderful girl Jessica had been. I did enjoy hearing people say good things about her personality.

Edward

I was only ten when Justin was born with a brain disorder. I remember him in the hospital, hooked up to tubes, where he spent most of his first year. When he came home, we had to have a nurse come in to give us assistance. Sometimes, I would help take *care of Justin. We were surprised that he lived for five years, especially because he required so much care and assistance.*

One day, after he died, I was outside in my neighborhood and a neighbor asked me how my brother was doing. I told him that he had died. The man said that his death was good because he had given my family so much trouble being alive. His comment really hurt. He wasn't the only one. I often heard similar remarks. I didn't like it when people would express those sentiments. Finally, I began explaining that he was just fine. If they didn't know he had died, I never told them.

Reminders

Yvette

My little brother and I were very close. Every Saturday I took him to a matinee at the theater where I worked. The first Saturday after his death, we were busy with the funeral. Then, the following Saturday I was in my bed waiting for him to come running into my room to wake me just like he'd always done. I looked over at my clock, and it was 10:30 AM. First, I started to think he had forgotten, and then it hit me—he was dead.

I felt so empty and lost. I remembered how I had been upset the last morning he came into my room and pounced wildly on my bed. Sometimes, it was a real pain to have to put up with him. Now all I wanted was to have him run through my door.

It hurt so much to see other little children coming and going with their families. I didn't want to begin crying so I worked diligently to be friendly to all the children. I tried to give to them what I couldn't give to my brother. It made me feel better when I could make a child smile. It felt like I had made my brother smile.

Sometimes, after time has passed and you are able to return to your previous routine, you might consider the value of replacement relationships, such as those that may be found working within your community or school. For example, if you long for the special connection that you had with your little brother or sister, you may want to consider volunteering with a group such as Big Brothers, Big Sisters, or the Boy Scouts or Girl Scouts. You may also want to offer your assistance as a baby-sitter, a tutor, or a teacher's assistant. Start an after-school program in your school for others who have experienced the loss of a sibling. Build a community garden. Help others learn to create Web sites. Volunteer your time for an afternoon in your local hospital's children's ward. Mentoring in your community will not only help you through your own loss, it will also allow you to assist in the development of younger children who need your support.

Starting Your Own Support Group

The best way to begin your own support group is to reach out to other area schools that may know of teens who are grieving. New friendships are often fragile. Ask teachers or counselors to sit in during meetings to help keep your group focused. Set responsible time limits. Respect others' individuality with an open, honest, and nonjudgmental ear. Realize that you or your friends may grieve in spurts, crying one moment and laughing the next. Networking in a group will allow each person to find his or her own constructive method of effectively dealing with loss, whether through sports, music, art, poetry, or dance. Most important, everyone needs options. A local support group filled with encouraging friends who accept each other's methods will help the grieving process begin.

Personal Items of Your Sibling

Your sibling's personal items are reminders that will need to be handled by you and your family. Some families like to keep their loved one's things exactly how they were when the person was alive. Other families remove items immediately. Your parents will probably be the adults who decide what to do with your sibling's things, but there may be some items that you would like to keep. Now is the time to express your wishes.

You may want to make a memorial to your brother or sister with some of his or her things. This will help you as you cope with your loss. Perhaps you would like to put some of these items in a special place where you can easily look at them, or place small items that you both shared at the gravesite.

Another choice is to use some of your sibling's things. This is a way of keeping your brother or sister closer to you. Sometimes teenagers choose to wear their sibling's clothing after they die. You may enjoy playing with his or her sports equipment or using her cosmetics. Objects have the value we give to them. Sometimes, it makes us feel closer to the deceased if we keep some of his or her belongings in our everyday lives.

Returning to School

Because returning to school is challenging after the death of a sibling, a family member can inform the school of your loss prior to your return to class if you wish.

For teenagers, school is more than academics. There are also the social aspects of being an adolescent. The death of your sibling has made you a different person. In some cases, you will be the focus of attention, which you may not want.

After you have experienced the loss of someone you love, you will be more sensitive to the topic of death. Some subjects, such as war and violence, may become more disturbing for you. You will find yourself offended by the lighthearted approach that many of your friends use when discussing death.

If you find something offensive, speak up. You may not be able to stop the speaker, but you will have shared your thoughts, which is positive and healthy. Many times, we do approach death in an insensitive manner. Your perspective is one that everyone needs to hear, even if it is difficult for others to listen.

Occasionally, grieving students aren't able to concentrate on academics and their grades begin to drop. This could be a source of distress for you. If you have concerns about your grades, you should speak with your teachers or school counselor. Schoolwork requires much effort, and with the recent loss of your brother or sister, your energies are being directed toward grieving. It is acceptable if you require some additional assistance with your studies during this healing process.

Your teachers may become alarmed if your grades drop. If they are aware of your loss, however, they may fear that you are having difficulty dealing with the death. This is not always true. Your school grades are not necessarily a measure of how well you are coping with the loss of your sibling. Over time, you will return to your normal performance level.

Some students' behavior becomes disruptive when they return to school after a death. This is a normal reaction, however unacceptable. If your behavior is disruptive or hurtful to others, you may need to seek counseling.

It is very normal for a person to perform at less than his or her usual level after losing a loved one. Do not give up on your education. Keep attending classes even if you find it difficult. Some teenagers have found that involvement with school activities helps soothe the pain.

April

I loved my nine-month-old sister, Lindsey. I was really emotionally torn when she choked on a small toy and died. I couldn't pay attention to my teachers, and my grades dropped. Later, I found that school was the one place I could go and get away from my pain. I auditioned for a part in the spring play, and when I got it, I was so excited. I worked very hard and everyone thought I did a great job.

I think the play helped me a lot. I did it for Lindsey. I felt like she was watching, and I imagined her smiling and laughing. We even wrote a dedication to her in the program.

Sometimes, you may even find that your brother's or sister's death encourages you to excel in your schoolwork. Most teenagers find that there is some change in their academic standings after they lose someone they love.

Rosa

> *My brother was a sophomore when I was a senior; we went to the same high school. He was never very popular in class. But after a drunk driver killed him, my late brother became a topic of conversation among my peers.*
>
> *After he was killed, all these people at school kept coming up to me and telling me how sorry they were that he had died. I would hear kids in the hallway talking about the accident. These people didn't even know my brother before he died. I hated it when they would tell me how sorry they were. It was so false.*

Special Days

Holidays, birthdays, family events, and the anniversary of your brother's or sister's death will be very painful and may increase your anxiety. These days are unavoidable, but you can prepare for them.

When contemplating the special occasion, include supportive people who are close to you, such as friends, relatives, or friends of your deceased sibling. They should be people with whom you are able to openly express your feelings.

Special occasions can be a time when you perform some type of remembrance ritual, such as lighting a candle or planting a tree in your sibling's honor. Sometimes, our actions of remembrance can be as simple as telling stories, watching videos, or gathering together to view the family album. As the years go by, you may change old customs and begin new ways of celebrating these moments.

At times, each one of us feels that we would like others to be absorbed in our suffering. One of the cruelest realities of coping with your loss is that the rest of the world is continuing as though nothing has occurred. Sometimes, you will retreat into your own solitude. Other days you won't do anything but survive your pain. Don't allow yourself to withdraw completely. It may feel painful to watch others enjoying life while you are hurting, but death is a part of life's natural cycle.

My Family Seems Different

The death of a sibling will bring many changes to your family. Many times parents are absorbed, overwhelmed, and neglectful of their living children. Living siblings are often forgotten, left to deal with their pain alone. Other adults may be busy tending to the needs of the parents of the deceased.

For many teenagers, it is the first time they see their fathers cry. After having lost a child, parents often become overly protective of their living children and begin to restrict their activities.

It is difficult for immediate family members to be supportive of each other through a time of grieving. Living siblings may find that they are caught up in disagreements with each other more frequently. Parents are often very stressed and can become more frustrated with the actions of the surviving children. In the most severe cases, parents choose divorce as an option after they have lost a child.

Sometimes, remaining siblings have difficulty accepting each other's situation. Often, the surviving siblings don't find comfort in each other. If this situation is happening to you, know that it is normal. Neither you nor your other siblings are wrong or bad.

You may find that your relationship with your living brothers and sisters changes in a positive way. Sometimes, brothers and sisters will be drawn closer together.

Adolescence is an especially difficult time to lose a family member because it is a time when teenagers begin to pull away from their families. Teenagers are establishing their own identity. This often means spending less time with family and more time with friends.

At the time of your brother's or sister's death, you may feel torn between your need for family support and closeness, and your need for independence. There may be family members who are critical of you because you aren't demonstrating the closeness to the family that they feel you should. Some may see you as distant and aloof. This may make you feel added guilt.

Brothers and sisters have many ways of relating to each other, either by showing closeness through positive comments or arguing. It is important to know that those with whom you argue are most often the closest to you. If you have a stormy relationship with your siblings, other family members may be more critical of you now. You may even be confused about your pain because you didn't get along very well with your sibling. You have lost a relationship in which you shared intense feelings. Now, you will experience intense feelings of loss.

Jimmy
> *I remember when Brandon died. It was my senior year of high school, and our family was busy helping me select my college for the coming year. Brandon was eight at the time. He looked at the brochures for the different colleges and would*

make his recommendations based on whether or not there were any pictures of skateboarders on the campus. I think he found only two that met his requirement. I guess he planned to skateboard when he visited me at college.

A bear killed him while on a camping trip with our church. It was extremely upsetting for everyone. The leader of the group felt responsible. There was a full investigation of the attack. Because of the threat that the attack posed for other people visiting the mountains, the situation became highly controversial. The subsequent coverage in the news compounded everyone's emotions. My parents were caught up in the commotion for several months. They didn't have any time to cry or mourn for those first few weeks.

My parents weren't able to spend much time with me. The discussions of which college I would attend no longer took place. At times, I wondered if I would even attend college. It just didn't seem important after Brandon died. I resented all the attention that his death was receiving. I felt as though I had lost more than just my brother; I felt as if I had lost my parents, too. We had been a pretty close family.

I hated feeling angry. It made me think of myself as a selfish person. I understood that they were in pain and couldn't focus on me, but it still hurt a lot. I ended up choosing a college near our home. Even though it sounds strange, I wanted to be close to my parents. Losing Brandon made me understand the importance of family relationships.

Feeling Abandoned

Being alone with your pain can be very difficult because it often makes the grieving period more hurtful and frightening. As you grieve the loss of your sibling, you deal with feelings of abandonment. These feelings of being left alone can increase when you are not given the attention and care that you need.

Many people are not sensitive to the grieving of siblings because they do not realize the value and depth of the sibling relationship. Often, it is assumed that parents feel the most hurt when a child has died. This is one reason that siblings are left to comfort themselves.

As a society, we are beginning to recognize the pain people experience when they lose a family member. The unique relationship that you had with your sibling cannot be replaced. Although you're grieving differently than your parents, the experience is just as intense and overwhelming.

Karla

I was thirteen when my older sister died of cancer. Throughout her illness, my parents had ignored me. When she died, I remember trying to talk to my grandmother. She told me that it wasn't as bad for me as it was for my parents—I had lost only a sister and they had lost their oldest daughter.

I was very sad and lonely. Because I had looked up to my sister and depended on her for advice, I missed her terribly. She had taught me about life and the importance of staying true to your friends.

People would ask me how my parents were doing, but they wouldn't ask about me. I guess they were like my grandmother and thought it didn't matter how I felt. I didn't have anyone to talk with until I was fifteen and my friend's mother lost a sister. She and I would talk, and she told me it had been the same for her. It was good to find someone who understood.

Teenagers as Caregivers for Their Parents and Other Siblings

Teenagers are especially prone to being placed in the position of caring for their parents after their brother or sister dies. This often comes about as a result of extended family members urging the teenager to be strong and take care of his or her parents.

Lucia

> *When my sister died, my aunt and uncle kept telling me that I had to be strong. They said that I shouldn't let my mother see me cry. They would tell me that she needed me to be supportive. It made me so angry. It was as if they didn't have anything to do but tell me how to behave. I felt so alone. I was hurt that no one would let me cry.*

It is normal for you to feel angry when your feelings are ignored. You may even be asked to take care of others while you are hurting. If you find that others are expecting you to provide care for your parents, you may need to remind them that you are hurting also. Your family may not realize that you have been ignored. Make your needs known to the adults in your life. If the first one you approach isn't responsive, try another.

Jason

Our family was small—just my brother, my mother, and myself. When my brother died, my mother cried all the time. I hated being at home, but my mother didn't want me to go out anymore. She was lonely and wanted me to keep her company. Since I didn't want to see her in any more pain, I stayed home for most of the first year after Sean died.

I love my mother and wanted to make her feel better, but now I can see that I shouldn't have stayed home as much. My mother wasn't forced to go on with her own life. I learned this after I started to see a counselor at school who helped me to see that I needed to get out of the house.

After the death of a child, many parents become very depressed and are unable to perform their parental duties. The living children watch as their parents fall apart emotionally and become somewhat helpless. This can lead a teenager to assume a caregiver position with his or her parents even if not directly asked.

Natalie

There were five children in our family before Lisa died. She was older than I was, and she had helped take care of our younger brothers. After she died, I had more responsibilities. My mother couldn't handle much after Lisa's death so she would stay in her room.

I understood that Lisa's death was difficult for her, and that's why I was willing to help out so much. I came home from school and took care of my brothers. I did all the cooking and cleaning. On weekends, I washed everyone's clothing. Sometimes, I was so tired that I couldn't make it to my first class at school. I really didn't even have time to cry.

One night, after I put my brothers to bed, I just exploded. I told my mother that I couldn't take it anymore and that I wanted to be a normal teenager. She started to cry, and I felt so bad. We didn't talk about it again, but after that, she started to do more around the house and asked my grandmother to come over and help out with my brothers when she needed a break.

Can I Ever Be as Good as My Sibling?

It is very normal for people to glorify someone who has died. You may remember your brother or sister as being perfect. Parents will sometimes glorify a dead child or make comparisons between the dead child and the living siblings. This can leave the living children feeling as though they aren't as valued. You may find yourself wondering if your parents love you because it seems as though you aren't good enough.

Your brother or sister was a unique individual with many positive traits. He or she also had traits that weren't as likable. Your parents may find that it is easier to think of only the positive traits of their dead child. In some cases, the remaining children are pressured to be perfect. It is not possible for you to ever be perfect. You must also understand that your sibling was not perfect.

Christine
  It always seemed like my brother and I were completely opposite. Keith was good at sports, he always

brought home A's on his papers, and he scored well on placement tests. Keith was the "star" in our family, at least it always seemed like that to me. It wasn't as if my parents never rallied around my achievements; it was only that Keith was good at everything and I felt like I couldn't do anything.

Things worsened after Keith died. Even his death seemed like my fault. He was doing our mother a favor, picking me up after school during a rainstorm. I guess that he lost control of the car, but my parents searched for any other reasonable explanation—the bend in the road, the speed limit, the car's worn tires.

In reality, I know that his death wasn't my fault, but I do feel guilty. I feel as though my parents wished I'd never been born and that Keith was their crowning achievement. Since his death, my grades have slipped, I'm failing two subjects, and I've gotten into other trouble that has forced me to stay after school. My parents always say the same thing: "Keith would never disappoint us like that." I wish that they would stop comparing me to him! I'm just not Keith!

Finally, I exploded in anger one afternoon while they were talking about the track team's poor record—obviously due to the fact that my brother wasn't running. I wanted them to notice that I was alive, here in front of them, and Keith was dead. I was never going to play sports, pull straight A's, or be a perfect daughter. All I could say was that they should accept me this way or no way. Immediately they saw why I had broken down. Finally they understood how all their comparisons had hurt me.

How Many Are in Your Family?

For many, the question comes up over and over in the course of life: How many siblings do you have? For those of you who have recently lost a brother or sister, this question is filled with pain and confusion. For several years, you may even have difficulty describing your family. You may not know whether you should include your deceased sibling as a part of your family. If you choose to include your lost sibling, your listener may reject your inclusion. This can be painful, or it may make you feel angry. However, as time passes, you will find a response that feels comfortable.

Am I Still a Brother or Sister?

Perhaps there were only two of you and now there is only you. Some would agree that yes, even though you have lost your brother or sister, you are still a sibling. There is no hard-and-fast rule. You did have a living sibling at one time. The decision to continue to feel as though you are a brother or sister is your own.

If your situation is unique, such as being part of a multiple birth, you are still free to consider yourself a twin or triplet.

New Family Order

The birth order of children often sets the path for how they develop and the responsibilities that each child will hold in the family. The death of a sibling will mean that some responsibilities will need to be reassigned. Sometimes, you will find that you will assume a new family position after the death of a sibling.

No one can ever replace another person, and you do not need to fill the role that your sibling held. You are a unique individual with traits all your own. However, it may make you feel closer to your family if you choose to take on some of your late sibling's roles.

Together, you, your parents, and remaining siblings share special memories of your late brother or sister that should be enjoyed. Speaking about a loved one who has died and remembering your lives together is one of the most helpful methods in recovering your sense of well-being.

Sharing fond memories with your other brothers and sisters may allow you the opportunity to laugh and smile together. All wise people know that laughter is the greatest cure for pain.

Death is a process that ends the physical relationship with those who are still living, but it does not end the spiritual relationship. Your late brother or sister will always be a part of your life and a part of your family. You will find many ways in which you will be reminded of him or her and times when you will feel the person's presence in a very real way. Your brother or sister may be gone, but your memory is alive with the moments that you shared.

Murder of Your Brother or Sister

If you have lost your sibling to a homicide, you will experience additional anguish. Someone showed the greatest disrespect and disregard for the value of your sibling's life. Coping with the fact that another person ripped that precious gift of life away from someone who was close to you is one of the most difficult challenges to face.

Death by violence leaves the survivors with a feeling of greater turmoil, frustration, and pain than the death of someone by natural causes. Brothers and sisters who have lost a sibling to violence have a tremendous task ahead of them.

The killing of your brother or sister did not diminish the value of his or her life. You may want to plan a memorial service that honors the uniqueness and value of your sibling. This can be a part of the funeral or a separate service.

It is impossible to be prepared to deal with the shocking news that your sibling was murdered. Your initial reaction to the traumatic news of your sibling's murder will be shock. Your state of shock may be so extreme that you appear to others as if you are "holding up well." This period of shock will not last. Eventually, you will begin to experience the mourning process with a greater intensity and pain than had your sibling died of natural causes.

Some people can't accept that someone would take another person's life. There are societies in the world and communities within the United States where the occurrence of death and murder are commonplace. This does not change the fact that the family and friends will suffer great anguish when one whom they loved has been killed.

Letty

Someone was always getting shot in our violent neighborhood. Each week we would learn of someone's cousin being killed or that someone down the street had lost a brother. It seemed that the more it happened, the more we just went out and had a good time. Sometimes, we would even do things that weren't very safe just because it didn't seem to matter. We started to believe that just sitting in your living room minding your own business could kill you.

After my oldest brother was shot, we all tried to live a decent life, including my youngest brother, Johnny, who was only thirteen. He knew that there were problems, so he stayed out of trouble. He had many academic plans to pursue, such as applying to law school. Johnny would have been a good attorney because he always liked to argue. He was a good student who had many friends. We all had high hopes for him.

One night, he and his friend rode their bikes to a video store to rent a film. He shouldn't have gone. Johnny went into the store, and his friend waited outside. There were several men arguing in the parking lot. As Johnny walked back out of the door, one of them pulled out a gun and aimed it toward another man, but Johnny was the one who got shot. He died later that night.

After the police caught his killer, there was a trial that lasted for more than a year. Whenever I saw my brother's story on the news, I got angry. I couldn't take it. Occasionally, when I felt that justice was not being served, I wanted to go to the jail and shoot his killer myself. My whole family went to the trial. We presented the judge with a letter telling about Johnny and how much potential he had to live a valuable life.

The killer was found guilty and sentenced to life in prison. Sometimes, I believe that he should have gotten the death penalty. I wanted him to die like my brother. Then I think of his family and how they would suffer just like we have suffered.

Now when I discover that someone was murdered, I think about the family and how much they're hurting. Together with my classmates, I have helped to form a group against gun violence. We had to do something. We couldn't continue to allow random acts of violence to control our neighborhood.

Anger and the Desire for Revenge

You will experience intense anger and the desire for revenge if your sibling was murdered. These feelings and desires will be overwhelming and difficult to contain. You must not act on your anger in a destructive manner. If you do seek revenge, you will find yourself continually bitter and angry. There are constructive methods of dealing with anger and revenge that will not cause you or others greater harm. Chances are that you will further complicate your life if you act based solely on your emotions.

If you begin to lash out and become physically violent, you need to find a safer release for your anger. You may wish to speak with a therapist who works exclusively with people who have been victimized.

Find an outlet for your anger. Construct a target with a photograph or drawing of the killer. Tear the picture to shreds, burn it, throw darts at it—whatever it takes to completely destroy the image in a way that allows you to safely release some of your rage. It is not wrong to feel anger and desire for revenge, but you must find appropriate channels for the release of your feelings.

Sometimes, the desire for revenge can be turned into a quest for justice. Many people wish to become actively involved in the investigation and trial. Perhaps you will begin your own fight against violence and injustice. Anger has been used to fuel positive changes in our society. For example, Students Against Drunk Driving (SADD) came about as the result of a group of students losing two classmates in a drunk-driving accident.

Jackie

Kristen's last words to our father were "See you tomorrow." We never saw her alive after that evening. She was walking over to a friend's house to spend the night.

She never made it. Her friend called us about 9:30 PM when she didn't show up. My dad got a little scared, but we figured she'd get there soon. At 10:00, when she hadn't arrived, my dad began searching for her in the neighborhood. Finally, when he couldn't find her, he came home and called the police.

The police thought she was a runaway. My dad had to insist that she hadn't run away from home; she was missing. Two hours later, a police officer showed up at our door. Kristen's friend had come over, and my mom had come home from work. The police officer then realized that it was not a runaway situation, and he called for more help.

The police officers who came in and out of our house all night searched the neighborhood and put out a bulletin on her disappearance. By morning, information about my sister was broadcast on all the radio stations. Her picture was on the morning news, and volunteers started arriving to help with the search. I was surprised that so many people cared.

It didn't matter how many people helped search; Kristen was already dead. We kept hoping and believing that she would be found alive and unharmed. After two days, her corpse was found in a creek near our home. She had burn marks all over her body. She had been raped. The killer had strangled her to death. It's terrible to think of what she went through. I can't let myself think about it.

After Kristen was murdered, my life changed. The police are still searching for her killer. I never trust anyone. When I look at strangers, I wonder if they did it. Sometimes, I wonder if it was someone that we still consider a friend.

Sometimes, I'm too afraid to do much of anything. I used to spend time with friends and go to the mall or *the movies. Now I never want to leave my house. I keep thinking that the killer is going to come after me.*

I'm angry all the time. I hate the police for not finding her sooner. I can't believe that no one saw anything. Sometimes, I even hate my father for letting her leave that night.

I get furious whenever I hear of a murderer getting a light sentence. Because of my excessive anger, I'm seeing a counselor. We talk about my intense emotions, my fear, and my lack of trust. She is helping me focus on how I can use my anger constructively. Perhaps I will someday use these feelings for good, but now I can't even think about anything positive.

Regardless of the nature of your sibling's death, you will find that you can go on and enjoy life. Allow yourself time to heal and the freedom to experience all of your emotions, but always search for safe outlets for your frustrations.

Survivor's Trauma

You may feel consumed with horror as you imagine the physical and psychological pain your sibling endured at the time of his or her death. It is horribly painful to visualize someone we love being hurt in the manner in which murder victims are slain. Your sibling may have been sexually assaulted prior to the murder. This, too, is an unbearable thought. Your sibling may have gone into shock. This would have caused the person not to feel all the pain that was inflicted. He or she may have been able to disassociate from the experience. Some survivors of violent crime have described their experiences as though they were viewing the tragedy from a perspective outside of their bodies.

The murder of your sibling may cause you to fear for your own life. Even if you have lived in a relatively safe environment, you are now faced with great uncertainty. And although you weren't the victim, you may suffer from symptoms of posttraumatic stress. You could find yourself behaving in an especially erratic manner, such as jumping when you hear a slight noise. You may have nightmares. Many people also avoid the location where their sibling was murdered.

Fear that you will be killed is very normal after someone has been murdered. In some cases, even people who don't know the victim may have heightened fears of death after learning of a violent homicide. If you feel that there is any real threat to your life, speak with your parents and the police.

Sometimes, people will feel guilty when someone they love is murdered. You may feel that you could have prevented it. Perhaps there was something you think you did that allowed your sibling to be in danger. If you were not involved in the murder, then you are not guilty. We cannot prevent others from acting on their urges. Someone else took your brother's or sister's life, and you are not responsible.

Police Investigation and Trial

When someone is slain, there is an investigation by the police. This can be a very difficult process for the surviving family members. You may become frustrated with the length of time involved in the investigation. You have the right to ask questions. Learning all the details available can help you cope with the murder. You may also be questioned.

If an arrest is made, there will be court proceedings. The trial will be painful. At times, it may seem as though the killer will not be brought to full justice. If you attend the trial, you will hear things that may upset you. There may be details of the event that you were not told previously.

Some states allow the victim's family to prepare and read impact statements. An impact statement is a speech in which the victim's family tells how the crime has affected their lives. The statement describes what punishment the victim's family would like to see imposed and generally acts as a voice for the victim. If you choose to participate in compiling an impact statement, it will give you an opportunity to have your feelings heard by the defendant, judge, and jury. It may also give you a feeling of accomplishing some justice. It is important to remember that your feelings are valid, but the judge may not impose the punishment you wish.

Throughout the legal proceedings, you may have been distracted from your grieving. Both you and your family members may have difficulty focusing your attention on your loss because of several distractions, such as attention from the media or stresses stemming from the trial. Usually, individuals begin facing the pain and grief after the legal process is completed.

Feeling Isolated

As a sibling of one who has been murdered, you may find yourself alienated, or removed from the rest of society. You have gone through a horrific experience, but you feel that the rest of the world is continuing as though nothing has happened. Your anger may drive people away, and they may feel uncomfortable with the intensity of your experiences. This can cause you to feel very isolated and alone.

Isolation during your time of distress can make you feel worse. When others ask you how you are, don't always say "fine"; share your true feelings. If you are filled with sadness, anger, or despair, tell those who ask. Talk about your brother's or sister's murder. Speaking about the events and how they affect you provides both a physical and emotional release, allowing you to overcome those feelings of isolation.

Families who have experienced the horrors of dealing with murder in their lives have found support in talking with others who have lost someone to homicide. At the end of this book, you will find a list of national organizations that offer support and help for families who have lost someone to murder.

Sudden Tragic Death: Accidents, Acts of Nature, and Suicide

There are many types of tragedies that kill people suddenly. Destructive forces of nature can bring about the death of many in just a few short minutes. When there is a natural disaster of great magnitude, we become engaged in the suffering of people who may be thousands of miles away from us.

Automobile Accidents

Automobile accidents take the lives of approximately 115 people per day and are one of the leading causes of death for young people. Teenagers, prone to thrill-seeking, often tempt fate as they drive. Sometimes, teenagers take risks like driving at extremely high rates of speed. Many times teenagers are responsible for their fatal accidents, but not always.

Eric
> *It just stuns us when we think about the accident. Shawn was studying for finals with friends. It was late at night, and they had all been studying for hours. Shawn was tired and left the house to come*

home. He was making a left turn and ran into a tree. He was pronounced dead at the scene.

He didn't die because he had been drinking alcohol. It wasn't drinking. He had been studying. The police told us he had fallen asleep while driving. Someone should have known he was too tired to drive; someone should have stopped him. He didn't have to die. There was no reason for his death.

We just can't believe it. One moment he was alive and studying, and the next he was dead. He was my only brother, and we were best friends. It was senseless. Before the accident, I believed that if you did the right thing then you were somehow protected from danger. Now I know that this is not necessarily how nature works. It's all so unfair and random. It scares me to think how quickly any of us could be gone.

Airplane Crashes

Plane crashes take the lives of many people at once. Although airline crashes receive lots of attention, they take the lives of a small fraction of people.

You may have lost your sibling in an airplane crash. If so, all the previous news coverage of other accidents did not prepare you for the pain you now experience. You may be angry if human error caused the crash. You may find that you are afraid to fly.

Freak Accidents

There are odd accidents that can cause death that don't involve transportation, such as the collapse of a building.

These types of accidents are rare and seem senseless. We often think of them as freak accidents. If you lost your sibling in a freak accident, you may be wondering why fate has singled you out in this way. It is common for a family member who has lost someone in a freak accident to wonder why something so senseless took his or her beloved.

Guilty Feelings

In the case of a sudden tragedy, you weren't prepared for your sibling's death. It occurred suddenly without warning. You may wonder if you could have done anything to prevent it. This can lead to feelings of guilt.

If you were not directly involved in causing the tragedy, then you could not have prevented it. Your sibling's death occurred, and you cannot change the events that led up to it. Talk about your feelings. Someone who is not as close to the situation may be able to help you see that you were not responsible.

Teenagers often have a greater difficulty with survivor's guilt when they suddenly lose someone in a tragic manner. You may find yourself thinking that it should have been you who died. Perhaps you go over the death in your mind, placing yourself in your sibling's shoes during the last moments. Despite this awful tragedy, you must forge ahead.

Target for Blame

In most tragic deaths, the living mourners look to someone as a source of blame. This is a common human reaction that allows them to find a target for their anger. Not every tragedy is the result of human error or action. Whether you hold someone to blame or not, there is a great sense of injustice when someone is lost in an accident. If we are able to blame someone, then it allows us a sense of control over our circumstances. It is very frightening to realize that we don't have the control over our lives that we desire.

Natural Disasters

When grieving the loss of someone in a natural disaster, such as a flood or tornado, there usually isn't anyone to blame. Sometimes, this makes the grieving process an easier one. Sometimes, those who have lost a loved one in a natural disaster will not release any anger, feeling that they must accept what has happened.

Keeping your anger inside will wear away at you until one day you come to a point at which you find yourself looking up from the bottom of a long, empty well. Anger that is not expressed is often turned inward, becoming depression. Later, this can be the source of a lessened sense of self-esteem.

Accidents Caused by a Family Member

In some accidental deaths, a family member is directly responsible for the accident. This can be an excruciating reality that you may need to accept. If another family member accidentally caused the death, you will need to forgive this person. This process of forgiveness may take weeks, months, or even years. You may be the one who caused the death of your brother or sister. If this is the case, you will need to forgive yourself. No one wants to live knowing that he or she caused the death of a loved one. You may have the double burden of mourning and the guilt of your responsibility.

Bryan

Before I pulled out of my family's driveway, I looked carefully for my four-year-old sister. She wasn't behind the car; she was off to the side. I didn't see that her ball had rolled under the car, and as I backed up, she ran behind my vehicle.

Wendy was so special to me. She was my baby sister, and I loved her dearly. Wendy was the joy of everyone's life. I cannot cope with the fact that I killed her. When I go to sleep, I think only about Wendy. I don't think I'll ever get over it. My parents miss her so much. They try not to blame me, but I know deep down inside they do.

One year after the death of his sister, Bryan attempted suicide. Fortunately, his attempt failed. Bryan then began seeing a therapist. He worked with a counselor and a support group for the next year. After the tragedy, Bryan committed his life to working with children and is now studying to become a teacher. Bryan will never be the same, but with help and new commitments, he is finding that he can be at peace with himself.

Sudden Physical Failure

Most young people do not die from a sudden physical problem, unlike adults, who may die from physical ailments such as heart failure. But there are rare cases in which a child or teenager will collapse and die without warning. This type of situation comes as a shock to everyone. Sometimes, after the results of the autopsy are reviewed, it is discovered that the young person had a congenital defect that had not been diagnosed before.

Lewis

My brother was the kind of person who could make friends easily. He was on the varsity football and track teams. He could bench-press 315 pounds and squat twice that weight. He came home from football practice one night, collapsed, and died. It was very strange. We knew he didn't use drugs, but that was the first thought of the doctors who tried to treat him.

After his death, the autopsy showed a rare heart disorder that hadn't been detected. The doctor told us that the combination of his body temperature and the exhaustion from his football practice brought on his heart failure. If we had known of his condition in advance, he wouldn't have been allowed to play sports.

Suicide

Teenagers are at a time in their development when they are learning to live independently. Their futures are full of potential. In spite of this, teenagers are taking their lives at an increasing rate in the United States. In America, suicide is now the third leading cause of death for young people ages fifteen to twenty-five.

A person who is suicidal doesn't always give any obvious clues as to his or her internal struggles. You may have never known that your brother or sister was distressed to the point of wanting to end his or her life. In some cases, you may have had some warning, but you were unable to take any action to change the decision.

People who are suicidal are like a tornado—once they have decided to take their own life, they will run their course, leaving behind destruction and despair. When someone reaches the point at which he or she sees no reason for living, the person begins to see the world from a very limited perspective. Often, the individual does not see a way out of the circumstances and feels that death is a better alternative than the current situation.

Death by suicide is one of the most difficult fatalities with which to cope. You must come to terms with the harsh reality that your brother or sister chose to end his or her own life. You are left with overwhelming feelings of abandonment, desertion, and rejection.

As a survivor of a brother or sister who has committed suicide, you are a victim, too. You now must face traumatic emotional responses. These reactions will seem as if they are more intense than if your sibling had died from any other cause.

When coping with suicide, survivors often find that their greatest challenge is the need to learn why their loved one arrived at such a decision. This need to understand makes the grieving process longer than in other forms of death. In most cases, there is no clear answer. Suicide is not a single act; it is a series of events. No one incident pushes a person to suicide.

Jeff

My sister was a senior in high school when she ended her life by taking an overdose of sleeping pills and drinking alcohol. She didn't leave a note, and our family never understood what drove her to the point of ending her own life.

I don't know why she did it. We loved her so very much. Why? Why? I keep asking myself what I had done to make her take her life. She was so beautiful; so intelligent. Why would she end her life?

We all knew that she shouldn't have been seeing Bart. He had a reputation for abusing girls. Katie was in love with him and couldn't resist when he pursued her. After about two months, their relationship ended. Katie seemed okay. She talked about him as though she was glad to have him out of her life.

I can't believe she would take her life because of a failed relationship. There must have been more, but I don't know what. She was a straight-A student and worked for many charity organizations. She was so busy that no one ever noticed her unhappiness. It's confusing. How could we not have noticed that someone in our family was so depressed?

My mother blames my father for being too strict with her. She thinks that he had too many rules for Katie. My father blames himself, too. Now my parents let me do anything I want. They try not to put any pressure on me. I really don't even care about anything anymore.

Confusion and Guilt

Suicide causes guilty feelings in the survivors. You are not responsible, nor could you have prevented your sibling's suicide. You may feel that if you had recognized the symptoms of depression, then you could have intervened. This is not always true. When someone is committed to ending his or her life, the person requires professional help from a medically licensed psychiatrist or psychologist. Without intervention from a professional, there is little that may be done to increase the chances of survival.

Anger

With every death, there is a certain amount of anger that is directed at the deceased. In the case of suicide, the dead person is responsible for the death and the anger, pain, and suffering that he or she caused family and friends.

Your brother or sister robbed you of your shared relationship. Any anger that you feel is a direct result of actions he or she took. As in all cases with anger, you must find a safe release. Every emotion, even anger, is valuable to you because it is your own. However, experiencing a variety of emotions is much healthier than getting stuck with one feeling such as anger. Do not let your anger control your life.

Shame and Embarrassment

Some people believe that suicide is a shameful form of death. This belief often leaves the survivors feeling ashamed and disgraced by their loved one's actions.

You may feel embarrassed at times and may not want to share the nature of your sibling's death with others. You must choose for yourself how much you will share and with whom. Keep in mind that, at least in small communities of people, the truth will eventually be known. Some families feel such shame that they deny the truth of the suicide. Denial is not a healthy choice. Facing and accepting truth is the only way to heal your pain.

Some people have reported that others have accused them of saying or doing things that caused their loved one to take his or her life. If this happens to you, reassure yourself that no one person or action causes someone to take his or her life. A suicidal person is lost in his or her own world of self-destruction. These individuals believe that their problems cannot be solved in any other manner.

Each one of us struggles daily with life's problems. Some of us carry great burdens, but most of us do not choose suicide as a solution. Even though behaviors such as depression have recently been found to have some genetic traits, the act of suicide is not genetic. Just because your brother or sister chose suicide, it does not mean that you are predisposed to do the same. If you begin to experience suicidal feelings, find someone immediately in whom you can confide.

No Chance to Say Good-Bye

If your sibling died suddenly, you didn't have any time to say good-bye. You may wish you had just one more moment with your sister or brother to let her or him know your thoughts. Some have found that writing a letter to your sibling explaining everything that you would have said is helpful while mourning. You may never be able to see your sibling again, but you can grant yourself some peace by finding your own meaningful way to say good-bye.

Regardless of the nature of your sibling's death, you will find that you can continue to enjoy life. Allow yourself time to heal and the freedom to experience all of your emotions. Always look for and use safe outlets for your frustrations, such as engaging in physical sports like karate or kickboxing, or creative pursuits like writing or painting. Consider these activities as providers of internal pride, bridging the gap between pain and acceptance.

Long-Term Illnesses, Including AIDS

Living with a sibling who is terminally ill puts a strain on all family members. If your brother or sister was ill for a prolonged period of time, then you have lived with the knowledge that he or she would die sooner or later. It is possible you watched each stage of a terminal illness in progress. This process has prepared you for the death that you have experienced and has made coping with that death a little easier. You may have been able to care for and love your sibling up until the last moments of his or her life.

Your parents' attention may have been focused on your sibling for a long period of time. Throughout the illness, you may have even been left to take care of yourself. If you felt jealous over the attention your ill sibling was receiving, you may have even become angry with him or her.

At times, you may have resented your sibling because the illness disrupted your life. You may have wished that your brother or sister would die quickly. These wishes and feelings are not wrong. Any feelings that you had about the situation had no effect on the final outcome of death.

The death of your sibling may have brought you some relief and, with that relief, guilt. It is normal to feel relief when someone who has been ill for a long time dies. All the changes that take place in the home, in addition to having to cope with a long-term illness, can make every family feel some sense of relief after the person dies.

You may feel as if a burden has been lifted from you. Caring for someone who is ill is an overwhelming task. In many cases, siblings of terminally ill persons have become emotionally exhausted.

Marisol

My little sister was born prematurely with an under-developed heart and lungs. She was never healthy and always required care. I remember the days when she would laugh and smile at the smallest things, like when our father spilled the pancake batter on the floor. Crystal started laughing so hard; she was like that. She made all of us laugh. She would smile, and everyone in the room would smile with her.

Crystal spent much of her life in hospitals. Everyone responded to her. She was very special.

Crystal and I were very close. I was thirteen when she was born. My mother had some tests done when she was pregnant so we were aware of her compli-cated condition before she was born. I remember being afraid of having a baby sister who wasn't physically normal. After she was born, though, I fell in love with her and committed myself to being the best sister that I could be.

I helped out with caring for Crystal, and she bonded with me. By the time she was three, she would crawl out of her bed and sleep with me during the night. My mother encouraged me to get more involved with activities at school, assuring me that it was okay to have my own life.

I became a cheerleader and a photographer for the school newspaper and yearbook. Sometimes, I missed a game if Crystal was ill. Photography was a good choice because I could do it alone and on a flexible schedule. I didn't have time to go out with friends.

I remember the day Crystal died. I had just started working. My cousin came to my job and told me that I needed to go to the hospital. I knew then that Crystal had died. She had been very sick for several weeks. I was relieved. It felt like a burden had been lifted from my life. I loved her, but it was a relief to know that she was now gone and no longer suffering.

It may be challenging for you to work through your feelings of grief while learning to enjoy new freedoms after the death of a family member. Sharing positive feelings with your parents may be difficult.

During the teen years, it is normal to pull away from your parents and siblings and begin establishing relationships outside of the family. Most teenagers are involved with friends their own age and participate in social events and extracurricular activities. You may not have been able to pursue an active social life during the time of your sibling's illness.

It may take some time before you are ready to pursue activities with your peers because you have become accustomed to caring for your sibling. You may have spent a lot of time with doctors and in conversations regarding your brother's or sister's treatment. You may now be afraid to venture out into the world.

After investing your time and energy in your sibling's illness, it is very normal for you to feel somewhat apprehensive about relating to others. You have gained knowledge about issues and difficulties that most of your friends have not experienced. If you are sensing difficulty relating to your peers, you may want to talk with an adult or a close friend.

Art Therapy

Like most creative endeavors, creating art can help a person let go of pain and develop a part of himself or herself. Creative expression is often the only outlet that some young people have to cope with all of the emotions that come with their first experiences with death and dying.

For thousands of years, people of every culture have been turning their grief into art and memorializing those they loved in paintings, sculptures, music, drawings, or writing. And, like others, you can also ease your pain by revealing your love of family through art.

Caring for Your Brother or Sister at Home

In some families, the child who was sick may have been at home all the time—during the illness and up to the last few days of his or her life. Your sibling may have died at home. This may be a time when members of a family draw together and support each other. It may have been a time when you were able to reminisce with your family, saying good-bye in a way that was meaningful and special for both you and them.

During the last weeks and days of your sibling's life, you may have noticed that he or she grew somewhat distant and withdrew from you and others. This may have felt like rejection. It was not. This was your sibling's demonstration of the knowledge and acceptance of his or her coming death. As he or she began to prepare for death, your sister or brother needed to close connections with loved ones.

Perhaps you began to grow emotionally distant from your brother or sister as you watched him or her grow increasingly sick. This, too, was very normal. You may have started spending less time around the person, beginning the process of letting go.

AIDS/HIV

Sometimes, if there is a great deal of shame or fear when people mention that their sibling died as a result of AIDS (acquired immunodeficiency syndrome), it is because they are uneducated about the facts. As more people understand AIDS and HIV, the irrational fears surrounding the disease will disappear.

You may have feared that you could become ill with HIV. If your brother or sister had AIDS, you may have been cut off from people and activities. Your family may have felt a great deal of prejudice and hatred. You may have not wanted to tell others that your brother or sister had AIDS. Many times, the best assistance for the victim's surviving family members is to join an AIDS organization or support group. Speaking openly with others who have experienced similar hardships is a good way to alleviate the anguish of dealing with the judgment and fear of others. You will find a resource for families dealing with AIDS and HIV at the end of this book.

Many people have behaved in hateful ways toward those who have AIDS. Because AIDS is transmittable, which means it can be passed on to others, people have feared the deadly illness and sometimes have gone as far as to shun those who are infected. For grieving families, this isolation is sometimes a cause for even more heartache.

Sometimes, surviving family members have found that there is little support or sympathy for them as they grieve their loss. Remember, people are afraid of AIDS because they don't understand it, not solely because they are making a judgment about you or your family.

Because of the ignorance surrounding how HIV is contracted, many families and individuals face extreme discrimination. Many people do not understand that HIV is transmitted only when the virus comes in contact with someone's bloodstream. This may have happened accidentally, such as through a hospital transfusion prior to stricter testing, or as a result of engaging in sexual intercourse or intravenous drug use. A pregnant woman can also pass the virus on to her unborn child.

It doesn't matter how your brother or sister became infected with HIV. His or her meaningful life was prematurely ended by a deadly illness. HIV is a reality, not a punishment.

There are families in which all of the siblings have AIDS. The illness was transmitted to them through their mothers at birth. In some cases, the siblings as well as the parents are infected. However, just because your sibling had AIDS, it does not mean you will have AIDS.

If Your Sibling Died When You Were Very Young

If your brother or sister died when you were much younger, you may not have had the opportunity to express yourself. You may have appeared to be feeling okay, but without the opportunity to express your feelings, you were not able to release your pain.

Perhaps your parents weren't open about their own feelings. They may have mourned and grieved without words in your presence. In spite of your parents not talking about their feelings, you were keenly aware of their pain and your own.

Your parents may not have discussed the circumstances surrounding your brother's or sister's death. Children who are not told the facts of their sibling's death can become fearful and distrusting. They fear that they, too, may die. Sometimes, they become preoccupied with protecting themselves. They can also become shy and withdrawn.

Jason
I was only four when Christopher died. He was just a baby, about three months old. He died in his crib during the night. I remember when I heard my mother

screaming for my father that morning. Shortly after, the firemen and paramedics arrived.

When the firemen came inside, I ran outside and sat under the steps of our trailer. I remember being very scared.

I could hear my mother crying and pleading with them to make her baby breathe. I heard my father telling my mother that she needed to calm down, but she would only scream louder. Finally, an ambulance came and my mother and Christopher pulled away. My father began searching for my sister. I was still too scared to come out from under the stairs.

When my father began to get angry, I finally came out. He drove my sister and me to the hospital, saying nothing. We were so afraid. The ambulance was already there, and my mother was inside. A woman came and took my sister and me into a room where we played with toys and watched television. After a while, my father came inside and told us that Christopher would not be coming home because he had died. Over the next few days, my mother just stared out the window and cried. Many people came to visit, but my parents didn't speak much. My sister and I weren't allowed to go to the funeral.

Later, I was terrified of falling asleep. I would scream and run when my parents wanted me to settle down for the night. When I did sleep, I had nightmares. My parents assumed that I was upset about Christopher's death. They didn't know that I was afraid I might die while I was sleeping. I was afraid my parents might die. If I saw them sleeping, I would shake them and wake them up.

I was afraid of anyone in a uniform. I thought the paramedics had hurt my brother.

My father moved out when I turned five. He couldn't cope with my mother's constant crying. No one spoke about Christopher. My nightmares continued until I started fifth grade. Then I began getting into fights on the playground. By the time I was in seventh grade, I had been suspended from school for fighting several times. My mother didn't know what to do.

One day a counselor at school spoke to me about my situation. Unlike most adults in my life, he seemed very interested in me. He recommended that I see a therapist. Although I didn't want to go, my mother insisted.

I met with a therapist for almost a year. I learned that I had a lot of fear as a result of my brother's death because we hadn't spoken about it. My therapist helped me become less fearful and understand that it was okay to cry.

Now, I rarely fight. I'm a freshman in high school and am looking forward to going on to college. I don't think college would have been an option if I had not found some help coping with my fear and sadness.

Jason's brother died from sudden infant death syndrome (known as SIDS). Because he did not understand the nature of his brother's death, he was left with many fears. He was not able to express his feelings when he was a young boy, nor did he have a chance to speak with anyone about his experiences. Finally, after his behavior had become very antisocial, he was able to find someone who recognized that he was expressing his repressed emotions.

Childhood Fantasies Equal Feelings of Guilt

As young children, many of us believed in things that are untrue. For instance, many of us believed in Santa Claus or the Tooth Fairy at one time! Sometimes, children believe that they are actually able to make things happen just by wishing or thinking about them. Children's imaginations can invent some fantastic creatures and stories. All of these beliefs are a part of the beauty of childhood.

Just as a wide-eyed and innocent child believes in magic and his or her own powers, children may occasionally even believe that they are capable of the extraordinary power to control things like sickness and health. These beliefs may be the source of a great deal of guilt if your sibling died when you were very young. You may falsely believe that you caused your brother's or sister's death.

Belinda
My sister was five years old when she drowned in my aunt's swimming pool. I was just about four. I believed that I had pushed her into the pool, killing her. After she died, I felt so bad. I would pray for God to forgive me. I tried very hard to be good to make up for killing Betsy. I never told anyone that I had pushed her into the pool.

When I turned ten years old, I couldn't take it anymore. I burst out crying and told my parents I was sorry for killing Betsy. My mother hugged me and told me that Betsy had been much bigger than I was at the time and it wasn't possible for me to have

103

pushed her into the pool. They assured me that I did not kill Betsy. They told me they were extremely grateful that I hadn't drowned that afternoon.

Childhood Wishes Can't Kill

It is very normal to have experienced moments when you wished that your brother or sister did not exist. It is normal to wish them away. Intellectually, you have now grown old enough to understand that you had no control over life and death, but deep down you may still believe that your wishes were powerful enough to kill.

You need to assure yourself that you did not cause your sibling to die. You need to accept that your thoughts about your brother or sister were normal.

Express Your Pain

Death is a universal issue that is often not discussed freely with children. We are now beginning to understand the importance of allowing children to share their feelings. If you did not have the opportunity to express your pain, you may now find that you need to release overdue grief.

Don't be afraid to talk with others about your loss. Begin to open up to people who are valuable in your life. Let them know that you need to talk about your pain and fears. Find a support group for teenagers who have lost a sibling, or contact an agency listed at the end of this book for additional help.

Some people will not be responsive to your need to express your feelings and your grief. They may feel that your loss is in the past and you should get over it. They may think that you were too young to be affected by your sibling's death. Your pain is real, and it needs attention. If at first you don't find help, continue searching. There will be someone who is able and willing to listen and be supportive.

Death as a Bridge

Now that you have faced the loss of a sibling, you may begin to see the world from a deeper perspective, a perspective that perhaps is not shared by your peers. Those who have not suffered a great loss are not aware of the anguish that accompanies death. You may take life more seriously than you did in the past. You may become annoyed with your friends, who approach life in their normal, seemingly carefree, manner.

I Am Not the Same

A change in perspective after the death of someone close to you is very normal. You cannot go back to seeing the world as you once did. The death of a family member is something that will impact your entire life. You may choose to allow your experience to help you develop a more concerned and appreciative outlook on life. For many, these attitude changes reflect a more mature personality and a part of yourself that may appear only after your loss.

You may feel an increased urgency to become involved with others. This is a healthy manner of dealing with your pain and bringing meaning to the death of your sibling.

Perhaps you will volunteer with a group that is already organized. Or you may be someone who will start a group that is dedicated to serving others. Teenagers have started many national groups after they have gone through a tragic event like the death of a loved one.

Not everyone who loses a loved one wishes to become involved with helping others. Instead, you may find that you want to devote your time to a personal goal or developing a new skill or talent.

Facing the death of someone close to you has brought you face-to-face with the fragility of life. You are now aware of how quickly things may be permanently changed. The carefree attitude that you may have experienced as a child is gone. You now understand that our lives hold no guarantees and we are without power over the forces that control our universe.

Who Am I?

When your sibling died, you may have begun to question your own identity. Your sense of self may have been reinforced as you were learning to understand your place within your family.

Your dreams may have been connected with your sibling because you shared a common bond like work or hobbies. You may have actually worked to assist and support your sibling to achieve his or her goals. At times, your brother's or sister's accomplishments may have caused you to feel jealousy or rage, yet you were proud of your sibling and his or her triumphs. Now you must come to realize that you are a separate individual. You can and will have your own life filled with personal goals, dreams, and accomplishments.

Why?

Death cannot be avoided. It will happen to each one of us someday. You have experienced the loss of someone very close to you. This pain of loss has permanently altered your life. You have had to deal with intense emotions. And now you may be wondering why. Why did your brother's or sister's life end? You may feel that there is no acceptable answer to your question. Understanding death poses some questions for which we have no hard-and-fast answers.

You will always hold the memories of your bother or sister close to your heart. And even though you will never have your brother or sister alive in your life again, you can turn tragedy into positive goals and ambitions for yourself and others. Sometimes, the meaning of death is found in the new beginnings that are created out of loss. Each ending can be a bridge to a new beginning.

Glossary

abandonment   Being left alone to take care of oneself.

AIDS   Acquired immunodeficiency syndrome is an illness that is transmitted into the body through contact with human blood, semen, or vaginal fluids. It allows opportunistic illnesses to destroy the human body until the victim can no longer live.

ambivalence   Having more than one feeling about a situation. Feeling both positive and negative emotions at the same time about a situation.

caregiver   Someone who takes care of another person or persons.

corpse   A dead person's body.

cremation   The process of heating a corpse to a high temperature until there are only small particles remaining of the body.

denial   A manner of blocking the truth of a situation and not allowing oneself to accept the emotional pain that may accompany it. Denial is often a first response to a death.

depression   An emotional condition that includes great sadness, feelings of very low self-worth, thoughts of suicide, and a lack of interest in activities and living.

disassociation   Disassociation occurs for some people when they experience great pain. The human mind is able to shut down the physical feelings of intense pain. The mind and the body are considered separated.

disbelief The refusal to believe in the truth; mental rejection of an idea or occurrence as untrue. Like denial, disbelief is often a first response to a death.

embalming The process of removing a corpse's bodily fluids and filling it with a liquid that will preserve the body for a brief period of time.

entombment A method of burying people above the ground in concrete structures.

funeral A ritual where family and friends gather together for a service honoring a dead person. The dead person's body is most often at the funeral. Funerals are held shortly after a death.

grief A human emotional and physical response to loss. It is a time filled with intense emotional pain.

grief therapist A counselor who has skills and experience in helping people when someone close to them dies.

hallucinations Things that are seen or heard that aren't a part of reality.

HIV Human immunodeficiency virus is a virus that enters the body and slowly begins to destroy the immune system. HIV-positive people will most likely develop full-blown AIDS.

impact statement A letter written by the surviving family members of a murder victim. This letter informs the judge about how they have been impacted by the murder. It can also tell the judge about the victim.

memorial service A service that honors a dead person. This can be done at any time after the person has died, even years later. The body is not at the service.

mourning A state of being in emotional pain after the death of someone close. It may include certain traditional rituals.

natural causes Death that occurs from an illness or is due to the impact of old age.

phenomenon A circumstance or event that is observed by someone.

rape   Forced sexual intercourse.

revenge   The act of hurting someone in return for pain that he or she has caused.

self-esteem   How someone feels about himself or herself.

shock   A physical and mental reaction to a traumatic event. The body slows down many of its systems while allowing the mind to accept the reality of the trauma.

solitude   The state of being alone.

support group   A group of people who have had a similar experience and come together to share their thoughts and feelings with each other. Most often there is a counselor who assists the group.

support network   A group of people, such as family, friends, coworkers, or others, who can assist a person when he or she is in need.

trigger   An occurrence in present time that causes someone to think back to a previous time. Often, a trigger brings up an emotional response.

vulnerable   An emotional state when a person is in need of help and comfort and can be taken advantage of by someone who may cause them greater harm.

withdrawal   To remove oneself from socializing with others and from many of life's normal daily activities.

Where to Go for Help

In the United States

Center for Loss and Life Transition
3735 Broken Bow Road
Fort Collins, CO 80526
(970) 226-6050
Web site: http://www.centerforloss.com

Children to Children
3922 North Mountain Avenue
Tucson, AZ 85719-1313
(520) 322-9155
e-mail: c2c@azstarnet.com

The Compassionate Friends, Inc.
P.O. Box 3696
Oak Brook, IL 60522-3696
(630) 990-0010
Web site: http://www.compassionatefriends.org

The Dougy Center, the National Center for Grieving
          Children and Families
P.O. Box 86852
Portland, OR 97286
(503) 775-5683
Web site: http://www.dougy.org

National Mental Health Association
1021 Prince Street
Alexandria, VA 22314
(703) 684-7722
Web site: http://www.nmha.org

The St. Louis Bereavement Center for Young People
692 Wyndham Crossing Circle
St. Louis, MO 63131
(314) 965-5015
e-mail: reveccab07@aol.com

Teen Age Grief, Inc. (TAG)
P.O. Box 220034
Newhall, CA 91322-0034
(661) 253-1932
Web site: http://www.smartlink.net/~tag

In Canada

Canuck Place Children's Hospice
1690 Matthews Avenue
Vancouver, BC V6J 2T2
(604) 731-4847
Web site: http://www.canuckplace.com

Kis's Griefworks, Surviving & Thriving
Canadian Mental Health Association
1400 Windsor Avenue
Windsor, ON N8X 3L9
(515) 255-7440
Web site: http://www.cmha-wecb.on.ca

AIDS Death

CDC National Prevention Information Network
P.O. Box 6003
Rockville, MD 20849-6003
(800) 458-5231
Web site: http://www.cdcnpin.org

Homicide Death

The National Center for Victims of Crime
211 Wilson Boulevard, Suite 300
Arlington, VA 22201
(800) 394-2255
(703) 276-2880
Web site: http://www.ncvc.org

National Organization for Victim Assistance (NOVA)
1757 Park Road NW
Washington, DC 20010
(800) 879-6682 (twenty-four-hour hotline)
(202) 232-6682
Web site: http://www.try-nova.org

Suicide Death

American Foundation for Suicide Prevention
120 Wall Street, 22nd Floor
New York, NY 10005
(888) 333-AFSP (2377)
(212) 363-3500
Web site: http://www.afsp.org

Resources on the Internet

Grief Recovery Online
http://www.groww.com

Julie's Place: A Web Site for Bereaved Siblings
http://www.juliesplace.com

The Layman's Guide to Death and Dying
http://www.bereavement.org/teen.htm

Practical Grief Resources
http://www.indiana.edu/~hperf558/res_prac.html

For Further Reading

Bode, Janet. *Death Is Hard to Live With: Teenagers Talk About How They Cope with Loss.* New York: Delacorte Press, 1993.

Digiulio, Robert, and Rachel Kranz. *Straight Talk About Death and Dying.* New York: Facts on File, Inc., 1995.

Donnelly, Katherine Fair. *Recovering from the Loss of a Loved One to AIDS.* New York: St. Martin's Press, 1994.

———. *Recovering from the Loss of a Sibling.* New York: Dodd Mead & Company, 1988.

Gootman, Marilyn E. *When a Friend Dies: A Book for Teens About Grieving and Healing.* Minneapolis, MN: Free Spirit Publishing Inc., 1994.

Gravelle, Karen, and Charles Haskins. *Teenagers Face to Face with Bereavement.* Englewood Cliffs, NJ: Julian Messner, 1989.

Grollman, Earl A. *Straight Talk About Death for Teenagers: How to Cope with Losing Someone You Love.* Boston: Beacon Press, 1993.

Heegaard, Marge Eaton. *Coping with Death and Grief.* Minneapolis, MN: Lerner Publications Company, 1990.

Kubler-Ross, Elisabeth. *On Death and Dying.* New York: Scribner, 1997.

Manning, Doug. *Don't Take My Grief Away: What to Do When You Lose a Loved One.* San Francisco: Harper & Row, 1984.

Raab, Robert A. *Coping with Death*. New York: The Rosen Publishing Group, Inc., 1989.

Spies, Karen. *Everything You Need to Know About Grieving*. New York: The Rosen Publishing Group, Inc.,1997.

Waldman, Jackie. *Teens with the Courage to Give: Young People Who Triumphed over Tragedy and Volunteered to Make a Difference*. Berkeley, CA: Conari Press, 2000.

Index